Stand Up Girl
Take Charge of Your Unexpected Pregnancy

Becky Fraser with Linda Shands

D0912467

SERVANT
BOOKS

PUBLISHED BY ST. ANTHONY MESSENGER PRESS
CINCINNATI, OHIO

Scripture passages have been taken from *New Revised Standard Version Bible,* copyright ©1989 by the Division of Christian Education of the National Council of the Churches of Christ in the U.S.A., and used by permission. All rights reserved.

Cover design by Cristina F. Mershon
Cover photo by Anton R. Casta
Book design by Mark Sullivan
Interior illustrations by Erik Simmons

Library of Congress Cataloging-in-Publication Data

Fraser, Becky.
   Stand up girl : take charge of your unexpected pregnancy / Becky Fraser with Linda Shands.
      p. cm.
   Includes bibliographical references.
   ISBN 0-86716-718-1 (pbk. : alk. paper) 1. Teenage mothers—Case studies. 2. Teenage pregnancy—Case studies. 3. Unmarried mothers—Case studies. 4. Teenage mothers—Religious life. 5. Unmarried mothers—Religious life. I. Shands, Linda, 1944- II. Title.

HQ759.4.F73 2005
306.874'32—dc22

                                                              2005016314

ISBN 0-86716-718-1

Published by Servant Books, an imprint of St. Anthony Messenger Press
28 W. Liberty St.
Cincinnati, OH 45202
www.AmericanCatholic.org

Printed in the United States of America
Printed on acid-free paper

05 06 07 08 09 5 4 3 2 1

CONTENTS

TIME OUT!

*So you're pregnant, scared and alone. I know.
Believe me, I know. I was in school when I found
out. People were talking at me from all sides. I just
had to take time out and look at where I was
standing.*

Hi, my name is Becky. If the above words are familiar to you, you've probably visited my Web site, StandUpGirl.com. Mine is the face behind the story. I'm there on the Web because I want to help girls like you who are going through the same things I did. I want you to know, no matter how bad your circumstances, that there is hope.

If you're one of the millions of girls all over the world dealing with an unexpected pregnancy, *Stand Up Girl* is for you. Both the Web site and this book offer a glimpse into my story as well as the stories of many young women who have struggled with the feelings, circumstances and decisions you're facing. We really want to offer you encouragement and hope.

Here is what one visitor has to say about the Web site:

*I just wanted to thank you. The best thing about
your site is that it doesn't have an agenda. It isn't
pushy or judgmental. You just provide stories from
girls who have been there and let your readers*

make the decision that is best for them. Again,
thanks so much for doing such a wonderful thing.

This book takes the Web site a step further. It will give you honest, factual insight into the world of pregnancy and reveal options you may not realize you have. You'll also discover you're not alone. The letters in this book are from real people expressing their real emotions as they share their real testimonies. I hope you can relate to and learn from their stories.

If you're dealing with an unexpected pregnancy, there's no doubt about it: your life will change. You can't go back. There's a baby growing inside you. You have some heavy choices to make. This book is designed to help you make positive choices, decisions that are best for you and your baby.

In the following chapters we will refer to other resources that can help you deal with a specific issue. You'll find a list of these places and materials, along with phone numbers and Web sites, in Appendix B at the back of this book.

As I think back over my own experience, I'm still amazed at the journey and where I am today. I thought you might like to read some snippets from the journal I kept during the early weeks of my pregnancy. Wow, does this bring back memories—both good and bad!

Purity is the one thing that I've really tried to
treasure all my life. My virginity is (was) the most
precious thing to me. Keith and I really love each
other. He may be the man that I will marry

someday. I want things that happen between us now to affect us positively in the future, but our passions took over, and I'm afraid I might be pregnant!

Please, God, give me the strength to handle the situation, whatever it may be. I am really scared. I called Keith, and he sounded scared too. I feel so alone. I know that you are right here with me, and I thank you for that. I need someone to talk to.

OK, so your pregnancy test is positive. The room is probably spinning, and your stomach is probably in knots like mine was. What are you going to do?

I'm sure you're thinking, "My parents will kill me!" Maybe you just broke up with your boyfriend, or he is a hundred miles away emotionally or physically, and you have no idea how he's going to take the news. If you're like I was, the tears have soaked your pillow, your hands are too shaky to push the buttons on your cell phone, and your brain is so numb you can't remember his number anyway. A surge of panic makes it hard to breathe, and you have no clue what to do next.

Stop! Take a deep breath. Before you take another step, take time out to think about where you stand.

PART ONE

WHERE ARE YOU NOW?

CHAPTER ONE

TAKING STOCK

OK, so I didn't plan on this happening. But could an abortion wipe out everything as if it had never happened? I had to think about that a lot. The truth is there is no going back, no matter what your decision is.

I'm not stupid. I have to do what's right. It was fear holding me back. I needed a lot of help, but once I started to look for it, it was there. Sure, I couldn't see what was around the next corner until I got there. That was the scary part at first. But once I stood up, everything changed.

Now it's your turn.

Where do you stand? Right now, this minute?

BIG QUESTIONS

I was twenty years old and in school—hundreds of miles from home, my family and my boyfriend. My period was late, and I was terrified that I might be pregnant. In the middle of class a wave of nausea would wash over me. Food didn't smell good anymore, and I had to force myself to eat. I felt so tired I wanted to sleep all the time. My breasts were tender and achy, and I felt bloated and crampy. But I usually felt this way before my period, so I kept hoping it would come.

I was so embarrassed and fearful; I had a constant knot in my stomach. What if I was pregnant? What would I do? What would people think of me? The questions rattled around in my brain until I couldn't think straight.

I wanted desperately to press the rewind button, to go back and not have sex with Keith. But of course that wasn't possible. How would I tell my parents? They would be so disappointed.

Yesterday was about the biggest day of my life: I found out that I am pregnant. My mind is full of many different emotions. I know I've offended God, my parents, everybody! I'm really afraid of how my parents are going to react, especially Dad. He is going to absolutely freak out! He'll probably disown me.

It's weird, but I'm also very excited. A baby! A new life! Lord, I can't believe that you'd actually trust me with this huge responsibility. I'm a mother. Wow! Keith's a father. Double wow!

I really don't feel ready for this. This new life is such a beautiful gift. I want my baby to feel wanted and loved.

Even though we are so far apart, Keith has been a great support. After talking to him last night on the phone, I'm going to quit my job. It's just too much for my body to handle the night shift. It's probably too much for the baby too. I have to start being more sensible and not taking on as many responsibilities that cause stress.

> *I hate to quit anything, but I will for the baby's sake!*

OK. Time out! Where do you stand?

ARE YOU REALLY PREGNANT?

Yes, you're feeling some of the symptoms, but you're still not sure. You feel as if your period could come any day, but it hasn't. I remember how my heart pounded every time I went to the bathroom to check and see if my period had started.

I knew I'd have to take a pregnancy test. I had heard that home tests sometimes give false results, so I decided to go to a crisis pregnancy center, where I knew the result would be accurate. Everything we talked about was confidential, and the test was free! (In the back of this book you'll find phone numbers to help you locate a pregnancy center near you.)

Of course, my test results were positive. The lady who helped me asked very gently, "What do you plan to do?" I burst into tears. I really didn't know what to say. I come from a strong Catholic background and do not believe in abortion. I knew that an innocent baby shouldn't suffer for my mistakes. Yet abortion did cross my mind as a way out. I was just so afraid!

Thankfully, this lady understood and let me talk it through, then explained all the options. Actually, I knew from the start that I wanted to keep this baby, but she helped me see that it was possible: there a way to do this.

There is also a way for you.

If you are pregnant, and even if you think you know what you want to do, please take time to really think it through. This book will cover the options available to you. Once you know the facts, it will be much easier to make the decisions that are best for you and your baby. And believe me, you will feel better about it afterward.

Shelly struggled with her circumstances, but she didn't try to handle everything alone.

Dear Becky,

I just found out that I am pregnant. I thought about an abortion and cried myself to sleep last night because I hated myself for even considering it. But really, what other choice is there? I'm eighteen and in college, my boyfriend comes from a conservative family, and we can't afford to feed ourselves, let alone a child!

Then I read testimonials from people on your Web site and saw that I wasn't alone. People from all backgrounds, all religions and all walks of life had to deal with the same hard choices I have to make. These stories gave me the courage to tell my mom, and she helped me realize that my child's future is as important as my own.

I'm not sure what will happen now that I've decided to have my baby. I'm still scared, but I know I've made the right choice. Thank you all so very much.

Love, Shelly

Where are you now? Are you away at school, living at home, living with friends or on the street? Do you feel too young, too old or too unprepared to have a baby? How involved in your life is the baby's father? What do you think his role will be during your pregnancy and afterward?

No matter where you are in life, please know that there are others who have been in similar situations and have made it. They found the strength to make good decisions and then follow through. Remember, you are not in this alone.

FACING REALITY

I would encourage you to take stock of your circumstances. If you've never kept a journal, now is a good time to start. When I wrote down my thoughts and feelings, everything became much clearer to me.

What are your needs, fears and questions? You wouldn't be reading this book if you already had all the answers.

Here's a prayer from my journal that shows some of the things I struggled with.

> *Dear God,*
>
> *I feel so alone. I know that you are right here with me, and I thank you for that. I need someone to talk to. Calm my fear, Lord. Please turn this situation into something good. Give me the strength, courage and humility to deal with this.*
>
> *Please bless my family and Keith's. It will be such a burden on them. Maybe I shouldn't go back home, but that would hurt them too. I really don't*

*know what they'll do when I tell them I'm
pregnant. I can't even think about it. It hurts
too much.*

And here are two letters from girls who asked for help:

Dear Becky,

*I'm sixteen, and I'm three months' pregnant.
My boyfriend is sixteen. At first I thought he
wouldn't want anything to do with our baby or
me, but he's been great. We are scared and
excited. We're not sure what's going to happen
now, but we've decided to continue with the
pregnancy.*

*The thing is, neither of us has told our
parents. He's sure his parents will help. I never see
my dad, but I know my mother will freak, and I'm
almost sure she will kick me out of the house if I
don't have an abortion. Personally I'd rather die
than have an abortion. I think I should face up to
my responsibility, but my mother wants me to go
to college. What am I supposed to do? Have an
abortion and keep my mother's love but feel empty
for the rest of my life, or have my baby but make
my mother hate me?*

...

Dear Becky,

*I'm eighteen years old and just found out I'm
pregnant. What a shock! I'm so overwhelmed my
head is spinning, and all I can do is cry. I haven't
told anyone yet. My mother will probably have a*

heart attack. I guess my boyfriend should be the first to know, but I'm afraid if I tell him, our relationship will fall apart.

I found several abortion clinics online, but I don't know if they're trustworthy. Believe me, I don't want to kill my baby, but I don't have much choice. I'm still in high school and don't have the financial stability to raise a child. Plus, there are many other obstacles that are too difficult to explain.

Becky, please give me some advice. I don't know if I can stand all this pressure by myself. I keep telling myself to be strong. I plan to make an appointment at an abortion clinic this week, but I don't know where to go. What should I do?

Wow, those letters were tough to read. My heart broke for these girls. We were all pregnant under very different circumstances, but we did have some things in common:

- We all wanted to please the people we loved, but we also wanted to do what was best for ourselves and for the tiny lives growing inside us.
- We all needed and wanted advice, not just someone's personal opinion about what we should do. We needed honest, factual information about our options.
- We all knew that the decisions we made in those first few weeks of pregnancy would follow us for the rest of our lives.

As you read this book, I would encourage you to use a notebook or journal to record your circumstances, thoughts and feelings, as well as answer some *key ques-tion* or *questions* at the end of each chapter. Below is your question for chapter one.

KEY QUESTION:
Have you taken a pregnancy test? If it was negative and your period still doesn't start, you will want to plan another test in one to two weeks. If the test was positive, now is the time to make some decisions.

CHAPTER TWO

IS THERE A BABY YET?

I grew up in a family brimming over with love for life. As the oldest of eight children, I journeyed through several pregnancies with my mom. I saw the sparkle of joy in my parents' eyes as they announced the news that we had a new little one in our midst. I pored through books with pictures of babies at every stage of development. I asked Mom, "Is this what our baby looks like now?" I gazed with awe at those little babies, so tiny and yet so perfectly formed.

I saw firsthand the innocent beauty of a newborn infant. I also watched my parents cry together over the loss of a child due to miscarriage. My siblings and I cried with them.

So there was never a question in my mind of when life began. I knew, even before scientists confirmed it to the world, that life begins at conception. I knew, when I found out that I was pregnant, that there was a baby inside of me—a new little life, a new little soul. It was such a beautiful thing to think about but also very frightening!

Have you thought about it? Do you realize what a miracle is happening inside you? You were probably taught the facts of life by at least eighth grade, but now you are experiencing them! Well, just in case you've forgotten the particulars, here's a condensed refresher course.

LIFE BEGINS

Every twenty-eight to thirty days one of your ovaries produces an ovum, or egg, which contains all of your genetic chromosomes, or DNA. The ovum drops into the fallopian tube and makes its way to the uterus, where preparation has already been made to nourish and cushion it should it be fertilized along the way. If fertilization does not occur, the ovum dissolves, and the build-up of blood and tissue designed to support a new life is sloughed off. You have your period, and the cycle begins again.

The sperm produced in a man's body contains his DNA. When you have sexual intercourse, sperm is propelled through your cervix and into your uterus, and it swims on into your fallopian tube. If the timing is just right, the sperm penetrates your ovum, fertilization occurs, and a new life is formed. Your genes and your sexual partner's genes unite to produce a unique genetic imprint of a human being who has never existed before.

At the moment of fertilization the DNA in that single small cell contains full instructions about that little person's gender, eye color, size, talents and personality. Will he be analytical or creative? Will she love to read or excel at sports? Will he scarf down his carrots but spit out his peas?

At day one he or she is already programmed with the talents to become a doctor, lawyer, carpenter, writer, swimmer, concert pianist, computer whiz or whatever in life. Of course, circumstances and lifestyle choices will affect this course, but the potential is already there.

As the fertilized egg continues to float through the fallopian tube, this tiny cell divides into two, the two into four and so on. Eight to ten days later the rapidly developing human being reaches your uterus and snuggles into the prepared lining of the womb. The cells of the tiny human organism separate into those that will form the child's body and organ systems and those that will form the placenta to nourish, enfold and protect the baby until birth.

Once the baby is firmly implanted, it secretes a hormone that helps keep the uterine lining in place for the rest of your pregnancy. The opening to your uterus, the cervix muscle, tightens like a clenched fist to keep your growing baby inside of you and protect that safe environment from outside contamination. Soon your baby sends out a chemical signal that can be detected in a pregnancy test. At about fourteen days after conception, you miss a period, and a few days or weeks later, your suspicion is confirmed.

You are pregnant; your body shelters a tiny new human being.

LIFE STORIES

At StandUpGirl.com we get many letters from women who didn't expect to get pregnant. All have different stories and circumstances, but you would be surprised at how much they also have in common. Here are a couple examples.

> Dear Becky,
>   When I found out that I was pregnant, I thought, "This is going to ruin my life." I wouldn't be able to go out with my friends, and dating

*would be out of the question. The baby's father
was out of my life for good. The only way out that
I could see was to have an abortion.*

*At first I thought of my baby as just a bunch of
cells with no life or feeling. But when I went to the
doctor and got to hear the "swoosh, swoosh"
sound of my baby's heart, I felt such
unexplainable joy. I couldn't believe that I had
almost chosen to end this precious life! This baby
was already a little boy or girl and was completely
dependent on me to sustain its life.*

*Suddenly I realized that my life had a whole
new purpose; it wasn't just about me but about
my child. That was the best feeling I've ever had.*

...

Dear Becky,

*I am now in my eighth month of a surprise
pregnancy and likely to deliver prematurely. My
instinct to protect my child is so strong. You see, I
know the feeling of losing a child.*

*I got pregnant for the first time when I was in
my teens but lost my baby at seven months along.
I didn't know much back then about how a baby
develops in the womb, so when the ultrasound
showed a beautiful little girl, I didn't realize she
should be moving around. I could see her clearly:
her knees drawn up, tiny hands and feet, a sweet
little head bowed as if in prayer. But she lay so
still.*

*The doctors told me then that my child had died
and they would have to "take it" because I
wouldn't be able to deliver her myself. Numb with
grief, I could only shake my head and cry.*

*A few days later they took me in for a D and
C. I can't even describe the emotional pain I went
through. I never saw my child; I never held her. I
regret that to this day.*

*I've been married now for six years. We have
two wonderful boys and seldom speak of the child
I lost. Right now the baby inside me, my daughter,
is kicking, alive and well and ready to join the
world. I anticipate her arrival even though she
also came as a surprise. Unexpected or planned
for, every child is a gift from God.*

Lydia

I can really relate to Lydia. I lost a child through miscarriage. I was only two months along, but I already felt connected to this baby. I had thought about the baby and what he or she would look like.

Miscarriage is not easy, and nobody seemed to understand. I cried for days. The doctors just told me, "Oh, well, you're young, you can always have another one." I wanted this one though!

After that miscarriage I had a whole new appreciation for the gift of life, its fragility and the tremendous privilege it is to be able to bring a child into this world. Like Lydia, I never want to take that gift for granted.

The psalmist wrote a poem to God. The entire work is recorded in the Bible as Psalm 139, but this is the part that

I especially love:

> *For it was you who formed my inward parts;*
>   *you knit me together in my mother's womb.*
> *I praise you, for I am fearfully and wonderfully*
>   *made.*
>   *Wonderful are your works;*
> *that I know very well.*
>   *My frame was not hidden from you,*
> *when I was being made in secret,*
>   *intricately woven in the depths of the earth.*
> *Your eyes beheld my unformed substance.*
> *In your book were written*
>   *all the days that were formed for me,*
>   *when none of them as yet existed.*
> *—Psalm 139:13–16*

Is that awesome or what?

It's also exciting that science has been able to show us the development of a new baby in the mother's womb. In chapter nine we'll take a closer look at what happens to your baby during various stages of development, and in chapter ten we'll talk about what's happening to your body. If you can't wait, go ahead and take a peek; the pictures are great!

But if you're like I was when I first found out, there is still some hard stuff to deal with—like telling your family, friends and the baby's father.

KEY QUESTION:
Take time to envision this little baby inside you. Is there anything you want your baby to know? Talk to him or her.

CHAPTER THREE

BREAKING THE NEWS

Telling people that I was pregnant was one of the hardest things I've ever had to do. I grew up in a strong Catholic home, and my parents had taught me how important it was to save myself for marriage. It made sense.

I didn't date much in high school. When I met Keith, I knew he was someone special. We got to know each other, and we just clicked. We loved to spend time together, and we could talk about anything. We shared the same values and had the same goals for our lives. He wanted to wait until after marriage to have sex too. But as you already know, it didn't turn out that way.

I decided to tell Keith first because I knew he would definitely be there for me. And he was. When I called him on the phone to tell him the news, his first reaction was "I'm a daddy."

After talking to so many women whose boyfriends freaked and took off at the news, I can see I was really blessed with Keith's response. Even if you don't think your boyfriend will be like mine was, at least give him a chance to step up and do the right thing. And if he won't be around for you, don't panic. Others have gone through pregnancy without support from the baby's father, and so can you.

Think about the people who are closest to you. Who do you think will be supportive? Even having one person to back you up can make a huge difference.

After telling Keith, I told my sisters. You could say I "practiced" on them before I broke the news to my parents. My sisters were shocked, angry and sad, but they were also very loving and supportive.

TELLING MOM AND DAD

My parents saw our relationship as "puppy love." They figured it would fizzle out over time. So when we told them we were pregnant, they were in total shock.

I recorded the events of that day in my journal. I hope that what I went through will give you courage to share your news.

> *The drive down on Friday went OK. I went
> straight to Keith's. It was so great to see him; I
> laughed and cried at the same time. I love him so
> much, but I felt sort of shy. After all, I was
> carrying our baby.*

Keith and I really were in love. While we didn't have money to pay rent, let alone support a baby, we were in it together, and we were convinced God would help us work it out.

> *Before we told my parents, Keith and I went to see
> our priest. He listened, and when we told him we
> wanted to get married as soon as possible, he
> prayed with us, blessed us and sent us on our*

way. The impending "doom" of telling our parents lay heavily on our hearts.

When we got to the house, my parents knew something was up. I started to tell them, but my tongue froze. Then Dad said jokingly, "What, you're pregnant?" I know he was trying to lighten the moment and show that what we had to say wasn't all that bad, but then I said, "Yes," and Dad's face went white.

Mom moved closer to me. She hugged me and held my hands. I was crying. Dad's eyes were flashing. Silence.

Then I just started spilling my guts. We couldn't justify what we had done. We wanted to say we were sorry for letting them down.

Keith started to explain how he felt—how he loved and respected me. Dad broke in and said, "You really haven't shown that at all in the way you've acted." He said he felt disappointed and betrayed. He said he felt like a failure as a father. I felt so sick inside. Mom tried to counteract his harsh words, but she had some hard things to say too.

PRAY, PRAY, PRAY

Most of you know you'll probably get some kind of negative reaction from your parents. Keith and I had expected ours to be upset. We knew they loved us but would be really disappointed in our behavior. Not to mention the fact that they still thought of us as kids and thought it was their job to make decisions for us.

It was my Dad who took over and laid out the
choices we had. He said we could give the baby up
for adoption to them or to someone else. Or we
could keep the baby, then get married later. In his
eyes, getting married soon wasn't even an option.

When he was through talking, they prayed
with us and we hugged, but things were still very
strained. Keith and I felt we shouldn't voice our
strong opinions then. They were still in shock, and
I really didn't want to get into a heated argument.

Someone once said, "Timing is everything." I found out
that's really true when telling your parents you're pregnant. Keith and I waited until we had made peace with our
own decisions and our own relationship, then we received
spiritual counsel.

When we went to our parents, we knew my pregnancy
would be hard on them, but I hadn't even considered how
many people would be affected by what we had done.

The next morning Mom and Dad talked about all
the ways this would impact our family. My
youngest sister was excited for me, but now the
oldest was really mad—she wouldn't even talk to
me. I felt like such crap! I went over to Keith's for
the day. We prayed and talked, but I didn't feel
peaceful at all.

Keith was the strong one right then. He told me it was his
baby too, and he would take responsibility for all of us. We
weren't sure how—college students aren't exactly rich—

but having someone assure me we would make it mean so much. Things got a little better when we talked to his parents.

> *When I finally worked up the courage to go into their house, Keith told them, "You're going to be grandparents." They were shocked, but they laughed and cried and hugged us. They told us that they couldn't give us advice. We were old enough, and they didn't want that responsibility. Wow! What a relief!*

Remember the time-out I suggested in the introduction? Keith and I had to take time out to get our feelings in order, to pray and to decide what to do next. My parents needed time out too.

Often, when the shock wears off and people take time to think things over, they are able to see all sides of a situation and make better decisions. Attitudes and emotions change. I found that out the next time I talked with my parents.

> *Boy, were our prayers answered! Mom and Dad told us it was our decision; if we wanted to get married right away, they would support us. They even offered us a place to stay after we got married.*

TELLING ACCOUNTS
Shelly, whose letter we printed in chapter one, told me her biggest fear was that everyone would hate her and call her names. But when she finally worked up the courage to tell

the baby's father, as well as her mother and her friends, to her surprise they were all supportive. Their support didn't take away all of her problems, but it sure helped her make good decisions for both her and her baby.

Anna and her boyfriend also found stronger parental support than they expected.

Dear Becky,

I'm fifteen years old, and about a month ago I found out I was pregnant. My boyfriend and I spent hours trying to figure out how I could get an abortion, just so my parents wouldn't find out.

We finally talked to his mother. I told her I was scared to tell my parents, but she persuaded me to tell them right away. She even called the next day and offered my mom someone to talk to. They didn't even know each other!

When I first told my mother, we both cried and cried. Finally she said, "Anna, I love you, and somehow we are going to find a way to get through this."

That day I went out with some friends, and while I was gone, my mom told my dad. When I got home, he put his arms around me. He hugged me for a long time, then with tears in his eyes he said, "Daddy loves you." Those were the most beautiful words I've ever heard. We had a heartwarming talk, and I felt a thousand times better after that.

Anna told her boyfriend first. They were both scared but finally went to an adult they felt they could trust. As it turned out, they were right about trusting his mother with the news, and her parents were even supportive. Yes, telling the adults in their lives was hard, but it turned out to be the best decision they could have made.

WHOM DO YOU TRUST?

Fran's story is different:

> I am nineteen years old and thirty weeks' pregnant. The father is someone I've known for years. He said he would support whatever decision I made, so I borrowed money from a friend and made an appointment for an abortion.
>
> When my friend found out how I planned to use the money, she demanded that I give it back. She was so determined not to let me go through with the abortion that she told my family.
>
> My parents were devastated. They pulled me out of college and brought me home. They were furious that I had planned an abortion and that they had to hear the news from someone else. Even now that I'm over seven months' along, they are so bitter that they barely speak to me.
>
> I really need their support right now, and I am not getting it. The father broke off our relationship, and even though they were once close, his family has not contacted us even once.

I am so resentful toward the "friend" who told my family. I feel like I have no one to talk to or confide in. I am sad, depressed and lonely. It would just be nice to hear someone say, "I know what you are going through."

Fran shared more of her story with me. She said that once she got it all out she felt much better. Sometimes just having someone to listen can ease our fears and set us on the right track.

When I look at these two opposite stories, I can't help but wonder if Fran's experience would have been more positive if she had told her family right away. It seems she trusted the wrong people with her news, and by trying to deal with it in secret, she discovered more heartache than if she had been upfront with those who loved her. Sure, they would have still been angry and embarrassed by her pregnancy, but at least the news would have come from her instead of someone else.

YOU CAN DO IT!

Anyone in a tough situation needs guidance and counsel. None of us were made to go it alone. We need someone to come alongside and listen to us. When we try and do it all ourselves because we're scared or embarrassed or we believe everyone will hate us, we usually wind up making things worse.

So think about the people in your life who will most likely be a help to you. Whom do you trust the most? Tell that person first. Then he or she can help you tell others who need to know.

It's normal to be scared to tell your parents when you mess up. Remember when you first found out? It took a while for the truth to sink in and a while longer for you to decide what to do next. Your parents also need time to digest the news.

If you can't bear to tell your parents on your own, have someone go with you: your partner if he is supportive, a friend or, if you're a younger teen, an adult who can stand with you and give you courage.

Keith and I went to our parents together. We had to stay quiet while my parents reacted to the news. Because we weren't rebellious or defiant, they eventually sifted through their own emotions and became very supportive.

If you're afraid to tell your parents face-to-face, you might try calling from a friend's house. You could say something like, "Mom, I'm at Karla's house, and I really have something important to talk to you about. Would you please listen for a minute?"

Be honest. You'll probably cry, but go ahead and share your feelings, then ask if you can come home and talk about it. If your parents need some time to work out their anger or hurt, ask them to call you when they're ready to talk.

Another suggestion is to write a letter explaining that you are pregnant and how you feel about it. Say the same things you would say in a phone call or in person, then leave the letter where they will be sure to find it. You can go for a walk or to a friend's house and wait awhile until you know they've had some time to adjust.

STAND UP AND BEWARE

If you're afraid of a violent reaction from your boyfriend, or if your home situation is dangerous, it's best to tell someone who has the authority to protect you. A priest or pastor, teacher, counselor, another relative, even a volunteer at a pregnancy support center, can provide a place to meet your boyfriend or parents where you won't be alone. A professional can help keep you safe and arrange a place for you to stay if you can't go home.

The point is that even under the worst circumstances, there is a way and there is hope.

Holly met a guy at the mall. He offered to take her home and she accepted, but when they got to his van he pushed her into the back and raped her. She felt dirty and was terrified that her family would think it was her fault. She was too scared to tell anyone.

Finally, when Holly realized she was pregnant, she told her best friend. Her friend's mother came alongside Holly and got her the help she needed. Holly's parents helped her press charges. Other girls came forward to report that the man who raped Holly had done the same thing to them. The man is now in jail.

Some guys slipped a drug into Sally's drink at a party. She had no idea what happened next, but three weeks later she discovered she was pregnant. She confided in an aunt, who helped her tell her parents. They pressed charges, and the father was identified by a DNA blood test. He spent time on probation, while Sally went to live with her aunt until the baby was born.

Milly was only thirteen. Her baby's father was a relative who had been sexually abusing her for years. She had tried to tell her mother about the abuse, but her mother refused to believe her. No one believed her now that she was pregnant either, and her mother kicked her out of the house.

She found help and a temporary home with a school counselor. After the baby was born, she moved to a foster home with her little boy. She will stay there until she graduates from school and can get a job to support herself and her son.

Whatever your situation, you do not have to go through it alone. Take time to make that list of people you can trust, then talk to them. Visit the StandUpGirl Web site, or go to a pregnancy support center. There is help out there; you just have to look for it.

I know from experience that you will feel much better once you have told someone. The stress of keeping that secret will be gone from your life. It will be hard, but you can do it.

KEY QUESTIONS:

How do you think your boyfriend will react to the news?

How do you think your parents will react?

Do you have a friend in whom you can confide?

Set a goal to talk to one of these people this week.

PART TWO

YOUR OPTIONS

CHAPTER FOUR

KEEPING THE BABY ON YOUR OWN

Many women choose to keep their babies, with or without the father's help. That's not really surprising when you think about it. God gave women a maternal instinct that takes over the minute our bodies tell us—in no uncertain terms—that we're pregnant. The new life is inside us, part of us—no way can we deny that.

Oh, sure, fear and confusion and a zillion other emotions can mask that instinct, but not for long. In fact, lots of women who've had an abortion tell me they feel that maternal yearning for their baby for years and years afterward.

Keeping your baby might not be the best choice for you, but it is an option to explore. There are thousands of women who have done it, and for most, it has worked out. So let's look at the idea.

I remember all the emotional and mental struggles I went through before I knew for sure Keith and I would get married. I knew I wanted to keep my baby no matter what happened. But I won't kid you; I was terrified. I knew it would be hard and that it would definitely change my lifestyle.

Keith and I did marry, and though our struggles have been bigger than if we'd taken a different road, we've also experienced many blessings. We are very happy in our marriage, and I wouldn't trade the gift of our child's life for all the riches in the world! Any sacrifices I've made have been so entirely worth it.

"OK," I hear you saying, "but my boyfriend disappeared the day he found out I was pregnant, and for sure, no one else is stepping up to take his place. I really want to keep my baby, but I'm scared. I'm in this alone, and I just can't do it!"

Maybe you can't, but then maybe you can! Remember when I said you are never alone? Well, that is true, especially when it comes to making a decision about what to do with this new life you are carrying inside you.

Oh, I don't mean it will be easy. Building a life as a single mom takes a lot of planning, but there are resources available to you that you may not know about.

FINDING FRIENDS

For starters take a look at Sharon's story. If anyone had all the odds against her, she did. Yet she chose to keep her baby and make the best life she could for the two of them.

> I was a sophomore in high school when I got pregnant. The father and I had only been together for a few months, and I soon found out that he wanted nothing to do with our child or me.
>
> I believed that abortion was wrong, but the thought of telling my guardian about the baby had me paralyzed with fear. I made an appointment for an abortion, but I just couldn't face it alone, so I begged my best friend to go with me.
>
> My friend's father is the pastor of a local

church. To make a long story short, she told her mom and insisted I come over to their house before we went to the clinic.

We sat in the living room for three hours while her mother talked to me about the decision I was making. We talked about the alternatives of parenting, adoption and abortion and the consequences of each one. It was as if someone turned on the lights and everything was clear. I made my final decision to keep my baby and be a mom.

My guardian's reaction was even worse than I expected. She called me every name in the book and wouldn't let me leave the house except for doctor appointments. Finally my friend's parents convinced her to let me move in with them.

I didn't know how I would support my baby or what our future would be like. Thankfully, the high school I attended had a teen parenting program. It provided parenting classes and day care, so after my daughter was born I took her to school with me every day. I graduated with my class.

It isn't easy to be a single mom. I can't give my little girl everything she wants, but she does have everything she needs, especially love.

Sharon

Sharon found help from friends and from the programs at her school. Some two-year colleges also have day-care programs. This is a big help if you need to get your GED or want to move on toward a career.

Kate's situation was more difficult:

Dear Becky,

I was seventeen when I got pregnant. My boyfriend and I had just broken up, but when I told him about the baby he said that he wouldn't abandon me. We tried to work things out, but everyone had a different opinion about what we should do. I wanted to keep the baby, and my boyfriend's father said, "Get rid of it!" My parents insisted I release the baby for adoption, and my boyfriend said he "had to think about it."

Eventually my parents decided I should go to a maternity home. I agreed but soon discovered that the home would only support girls who chose adoption. When I wouldn't follow their rules, they kicked me out. I called my mom, but she told me in no uncertain terms that I could not come home. For a while I stayed with friends, but I was basically homeless until my mom relented and helped me rent a house.

My mom was in the delivery room, and once my baby arrived, my dad came around. That was the happiest day of my life.

I now have a beautiful, extremely intelligent seven-year-old girl, a wonderful husband and a nursing degree. It hasn't been easy, but if I could beat the odds, anyone can. I hope this letter gives someone else the courage to try.

Love, Kate

LET'S GET PRACTICAL

So what will you need the most if you decide you want to keep your baby and the father isn't around? For sure you'll need emotional support from someone. I hope you've made a list and found someone who will at least listen.

If not, or if there is absolutely no one out there you think you can trust, please call one of the phone numbers in the back of this book and find a crisis pregnancy center close to you. Those people deal with unexpected pregnancies every day. They'll listen without judging you and put you in contact with others in your community who can help you in practical ways.

If you're very young or still in school, you'll need a place to live and some kind of financial support. Once their parents calm down, most of the girls I've talked to find some support at home and are allowed to live there.

If that just won't work for you, ask your support person to help you contact a social services agency in your community. Most agencies can help you find a place to stay. It may be the home of a friend, a foster home, a maternity home—though Kate didn't have a good experience at the one she went to, lots of girls do fine—or even subsidized housing, which means the government will help you pay the rent on an apartment. If you're totally on your own, that same agency will help you with food stamps or a financial allotment for meals.

Another thing you'll need for sure is prenatal care and a doctor or midwife to help deliver your baby. Most countries have some kind of subsidized insurance for this as well. Be sure to make an appointment with a doctor right away. And please be honest with him or her. If you've been drinking or doing drugs, or have some kind of infection or sexually transmitted disease (STD), your doctor will know how to treat any problems. Telling the doctor upfront will give you a better chance of a normal pregnancy, not to mention a healthy baby.

After the baby is born, you may be able to continue the living arrangement you're in. You may choose to stay in school, find a job or both! In any case you'll need someone to help take care of the baby during those times when you can't be there. School day-care centers along with supportive family members or friends will usually meet that need.

Crisis pregnancy centers and other community service organizations offer free maternity clothes, diapers, formula and baby clothes, as well as prenatal and parenting classes. If you plan to breast-feed, there are experts who can help you with that too. Other programs provide food during your pregnancy as well as food and formula, if you need it, for your baby after he or she is born.

You'll feel much better if all of these things are taken care of before your baby's born. So if you think you will be a single mom, please take time to check things out now.

Believe me, I know that keeping your baby will take sacrifice, determination and just plain old-fashioned work. Babies don't feed and diaper themselves. They sleep when you have to be awake and want to play when you need to sleep. They cry when they're hungry, wet or lonely, or just to express their opinion.

Crying is the only way an infant can talk to you—except for the coos and smiles and fantastic faces they make when they've found something new to explore. I'll never forget my daughter's delight the first time she grabbed and tasted her own foot. Or the times she stopped nursing to look up at me with that milk-sodden grin. My heart melted at her recognition and trust.

Your baby will throw up on your favorite white shirt or dirty her diaper just as you are headed out the door, chew on your knuckle when she's cutting teeth and drool down the back of your new sweater. And here's a personal experience alert: if you use cloth diapers, avoid baby foods such as spinach or beets. I think you get the picture.

But nothing smells or looks sweeter than a freshly bathed, powdered and sleepy baby. You can bathe and powder yourself when your baby is finally asleep in the crib.

Will your life ever be the same? No way. Is keeping your baby worth it? Oh, yes!

KEY QUESTION:
Is raising your baby the right choice for you? Make a list of the pros and cons that fit your situation.

CHAPTER FIVE

MARRYING YOUR BABY'S FATHER

Keith and I had talked about marriage in the past, so this wasn't a totally new idea. It would just happen a lot sooner than we had planned. I had to quit school. Keith got a job in our hometown, as we wanted to be near our parents. We felt that bringing our baby into a family was a priority.

Our parents were being really supportive, but my dad still had some questions to ask me:

- Did I love Keith above any other, *forever*?
- Was I willing to live with him and his faults and not try to change them?
- Did I know the difference between love and lust?

I answered "yes" to all these questions. I poured out my heart to my parents about my feelings for Keith and our plans for the future. They both looked quite choked up. Keith was ecstatic when I told him what had happened! Things were much lighter from then on. We all joked and made plans.

Keith and I were nineteen when we married. Keith was able to get a job, and we had our parents' help and support. I know that's not the way it is for everyone. Some couples really love each other and want to take responsibility for this new life together, but it isn't as easy as just saying, "OK, we'll get married."

AGAINST THE ODDS

Dee and her boyfriend were young when they faced this decision:

> My boyfriend and I were both sixteen when we found out I was pregnant. He was happy about it, but when we told my parents they blew up. His family wasn't as angry, but they all made it clear we were on our own.
>
> We decided to have the baby and take care of everything together. We both had part-time jobs and lived at home, so we had that going for us. We bought baby clothes and furniture from the Salvation Army.
>
> It hurt that my parents just ignored us; it was as if they were just waiting for us to fail. They thought the stress would drive us apart. Instead the shared decisions and chores brought us closer together.
>
> Then we found out that I was having twins!
>
> I suffered from morning sickness and depression throughout the whole pregnancy, but somehow I got through it all to start the next year of school. I had my babies, a boy and a girl. My boyfriend's sister threw us a baby shower and helped take care of the babies so we could finish our senior year.
>
> We were married as soon as we graduated. My husband got a job with a landscape company, and we rented a small one-bedroom apartment. We

*qualified for food stamps and stayed on state aid
until the twins were old enough for me to get a job.*

*My babies are eighteen months old and per-
fectly healthy. I'm so glad we didn't give in and "get
rid of the problem," as a lot of people suggested.*

Wow! Sixteen is young. And twins: That must have been a
real challenge. But Dee and the babies' father have made
it this far. My prayer is that they will be able to face the
other challenges ahead and stick it out together. Not easy,
especially at that age, but it can be done!

Mandy also was young:

*When I first found out I was pregnant, I was only
sixteen and so scared I thought abortion was my
only option. My boyfriend and I agreed to get it
over with and not tell our parents.*

*When we got to the clinic, I saw a pamphlet
with several pictures of aborted babies. I knew
then that if we went through with it, I would
resent my boyfriend and hate myself for the rest
of my life.*

*We had to tell our parents. After a few weeks
they accepted the fact that we were going to have a
baby, and everyone helped me out as much as
they could. Money was a problem, so I went to a
couple of local agencies that provided free baby
clothes, diapers, a bassinet and a car seat. A
federal program called WIC—Women, Infant and
Children services—helped us with food and*

*prenatal care. I stayed in school, maintained my
grades and even played softball.*

*When my baby boy was born, I took him to
the school day-care center for free. With the extra
help I graduated early. My son's father and I were
married six months later. I was very young, and I
know the odds were against us, but we managed
to make a life together, and I can honestly say we
are a very happy family.*

Keith and I married before our baby was born. Dee and
Mandy were quite a bit younger, so they waited until after
they had their babies and had graduated from high school.
Only you can decide what's right for you.

Theya and Tom cared about each other and the baby
they were going to have, but they decided they were too
young for marriage. Tom helped with the baby as much as
he could, but five dollars an hour at a part-time job didn't
go very far. They both lived at home, with Theya and her
mom mostly raising the baby.

When the baby turned three, Theya and Tom were a
little more independent. They had both graduated and had
jobs. They started dating again, and a few months later
they decided they really loved each other and wanted to
get married. They've been married for several years now
and have added two other children to the family.

ARE YOU READY?
I have to be honest: Marriage isn't always easy. It takes a
lot of dedication and commitment to share life with someone, even someone you love, and adding a baby to the mix
makes it even more complicated.

Then too, the younger you are, the more change you have ahead of you. At fifteen and sixteen you and your boyfriend may like the same music, hang out with the same crowd and have the same value system, but what happens when you are in your twenties and discover your values and emotions have changed?

He still wants to hang out and play poker with the guys, but you want him to stay home and pay attention to you. You think you are entitled to a night off, but he would rather watch TV than watch the baby. Or he turns out to be a neat freak and is constantly on your case about the dirty house, which you loudly remind him would not be a problem if he would help out a little more. Then he reminds you, even more forcefully, that he already has a job that drives him crazy.

And you just know in your heart, without bothering to ask him, that you drive him crazy too, and if he didn't have you and your child, all his problems would be solved. As for you, it would be easier to live without him, you feel all alone in this anyway, so why not do it alone for real and have a lot more peace in the process?

There are a million scenarios like this, and unless you can learn to communicate and adjust to the changes with a lot of unselfish give-and-take, divorce is a real possibility. My dad knew that. That's why he asked me those pointed questions when I told him I wanted to marry Keith.

You might want to think about those questions and ask your boyfriend to answer them too:

• Do you love him or her above any other *forever*?

- Are you willing to live with his or her faults and not try to change them?
- Do you know the difference between love and lust?

There is a big difference, you know. Sex is great, but it lasts only for the moment. Love is patient, kind and unselfish. Love looks to what's best for the other person and chooses to give up its own way to benefit the other person.

Love is for always. In a universal marriage ceremony each person promises to love the other "for better or for worse, until death do us part." From your teens to death could be a very long time.

Stella's story gives an example of a marriage that did not work, as well as one that did!

When I was sixteen I got pregnant. Some people told me to have an abortion, but I just couldn't do it. I dropped out of school, and my parents insisted we get married. I felt that I had no other choice, so I married the boy.

To make a very long story short, things were terrible, and he abused me. We were both too young to be married. After I left him, my baby and I saw him only twice.

When I was seventeen, and holding that little baby in my arms, I thought my life was over. I didn't realize my adventure was just beginning.

There were times when I thought that I could not go on. But my girl gave me the strength to take care of myself. My beautiful baby made me realize

*that I was worth something to someone, and she
needed me. I really feel that God gave her to me to
save my life.*

*I finally met the man I was meant to be with.
My past did not matter to him, and after we
married he adopted my daughter.*

*Everything I went through has made me the
woman I am today. I finally like myself and have
a family who loves me. My daughter is ten years
old and absolutely beautiful. Sometimes I have to
pinch myself to believe it's true.*

I know that having two parents is what's best for a baby.
But getting married just because you're pregnant may not
be the best choice. It might be better to wait awhile and
see what happens between you and the baby's father. If
you are really committed to each other and willing to sacrifice to make your marriage work, it could be the best
decision you've ever made. It sure was for Keith and me.

KEY QUESTIONS:

What is your present relationship with your baby's father?

How would that have to change if you were to marry him?

What are his strengths and weaknesses?

*How do his ideas about marriage and family compare to
   yours?*

*Are you ready to commit the rest of your lives to each other
   and your baby?*

CHAPTER SIX

ADOPTION

Keith and I knew from the beginning that we would raise our baby together. But if that can't happen for you, I really want you to hear from some of the girls who decided on adoption as the best choice for them.

Lots of girls say they would rather have an abortion than "give up" their baby. If you're one of them, you probably think it will be too painful for you to carry the baby to term and release him or her into someone else's care. You know that the bond with your baby will be really strong by then, and it would be easier to get rid of the baby now, while fear is masking that bond, than face pregnancy, delivery and the emotional pain of letting the baby go.

I can see how you might feel that way, but please take a few minutes to read this chapter before you decide.

A LIFE CHOICE

Candy's letter is too long to print, but I think it explains a lot about adoption and what it can mean for a single mom and her baby. She wrote to me, after reading several other letters on the Web site, so she could encourage others with her story. I'll try and sum it up for you.

Candy had just turned twenty-one when she found out she was pregnant. She felt she had three options: get an abortion, keep the baby or give the baby up for adoption. Her boyfriend wanted her to have an abortion. He wasn't ready to make a commitment to marriage, let alone raise a child. But as Candy put it, "I knew there was a life inside me, and I refused to end it for my own convenience."

With abortion "out of the question," Candy thought about what it would be like to keep the baby herself. She had been raised in a single-parent household and knew firsthand the trials and sacrifices she and her mother had faced. She felt strongly that her child should have a secure home with a mother and a father.

"It was a very difficult decision," Candy said. "I already loved this little one I carried inside me, but I had to do what was best for the baby and not myself."

After several weeks of research and struggle, Candy decided to release her baby for adoption. Her family supported her decision, but her mom cried over what she considered the loss of her first grandchild. Candy held firm. "I wanted to give my baby the best start possible, with two parents who would love him and have the financial resources to take care of him. At that time my boyfriend and I did not qualify!"

Candy felt a closed adoption would be best for all of them. If her child wanted to find her when he became an adult, she would receive him gladly. In the meantime she felt that it would be best to allow him to grow up knowing he was adopted but secure in the love of a "real family."

Candy found a lawyer who specialized in placing babies. The lawyer gave her an album with pictures and information about prospective parents, and Candy chose a few to investigate.

One couple stood out among all the others. They were financially stable and had the lifestyle and values that Candy believed would be best for her child. She wrote to them through the lawyer and told them things that she felt were important for her child to know.

"Please tell him that I love him so much that I gave up the privilege of raising him for all the opportunities a stable home could bring," Candy wrote. She had faith that his parents would eventually share those letters with him and teach him that he was very much wanted and loved.

Candy's mom attended birthing classes with her and was there when she delivered a healthy, seven-pound, nine-ounce baby boy. Candy had the option of spending time with her baby in the hospital or having the nurses feed and care for him until the adoptive parents arrived. She chose to get to know the little one whom she had nurtured and protected for a full nine months. She didn't name him because she wanted his adoptive parents to have that privilege.

The time finally came when she handed her baby boy to his new mother. "I told her I trusted her to raise my son." It was a bittersweet moment with lots of tears.

Candy insists that releasing her baby for adoption wasn't easy. For months she cried herself to sleep, and she wept every time she saw a family with a newborn. But she has never regretted the decision.

"I knew that, despite my personal pain and emptiness, I had done the right thing," she says. "My regrets are for having premarital sex in the first place and putting myself in that situation."

Candy's decision took a lot of courage! She had all the joys and the discomforts of a normal pregnancy. She heard her baby's heartbeat and felt him kick and push inside her as he grew. Then she went through the pains of labor and a long, exhausting delivery. When the nurse asked her if she wanted to hold her baby, she said, "Of course!"

It must have been hard for Candy to release her son after that. I remember when I saw my little girl for the first time. I looked into her eyes and just cried. She was so innocent and trusting and helpless! She needed all the love I had to give her and more: food, clothes and a warm, stable home where she could learn and grow. Keith and I were in a position to provide for her; Candy couldn't do that for her son. Her gift to him and his new parents was a sacrifice of love.

I know adoption isn't for everyone, but I hope Candy's story encourages you to give your baby life. God will give you the strength you need if you ask him.

FINDING A FAMILY

Tiffany found adoption to be her best choice. She wrote to Lisa, my partner on the StandUpGirl Web site.

> *Dear Lisa,*
>
> *I was fourteen when I found out that I was pregnant. I thought life couldn't get any worse. At first my mom said I would have to have an abortion because we couldn't afford to take care of a baby. The next day we sat down and talked about all the options. It was the hardest decision I've ever made, but I finally chose to release my baby for adoption.*

I chose an open adoption, in which I was able to pick the adoptive parents. It's an amazing, depressing and wonderful experience. I know that my life will never be the same again because I made a baby and she is out there in the world. But she will be in a loving home with two parents who can give her everything she needs.

I never thought that I would be a teen mom, but at least I haven't ruined my baby's life. I've only made it better.

Tiffany

Tiffany and her mom also went through an adoption lawyer. She chose a family in much the same way Candy did. The adoptive parents most likely paid the lawyer fees and most of Tiffany's medical bills. They may have picked up the baby from the hospital nursery, or a social worker may have arranged another meeting place.

There are lots of different ways to set up an adoption. In open adoption you not only choose your baby's future parents, but once you get to know them, you work out a deal about how much of a part you'll have in your child's life. I've talked to girls who went this way and decided to have no contact with their baby and her new family. Tiffany doesn't mention any contact with the couple who would raise her baby. Other girls see the baby all the time, and the new family pretty much adopts them too!

Cindy was fifteen when she got pregnant. According to her, she "freaked out," and so did everyone else in her life. She decided to look into open adoption, and with the help of an adoption counselor she chose the parents she felt could give her baby the best life possible. As she got to know her baby's future parents, she became really attached to them and they to her. Now she visits with them and sees her daughter often.

GOD HAS A PLAN

There are lots of stories like that, and these girls say they feel lucky. Even though they can't raise the baby, he or she is safe and happy with someone who can. One girl, who had no real support from anyone before she got pregnant, said she wouldn't trade her choice of open adoption for anything. She was able to stay a teenager, play with her baby like a big sister and feel like part of a family.

Speaking of family, I know of several girls who had relatives willing to adopt the baby. Sara was thirteen when she got pregnant. Her mom and dad adopted her baby, and now Sara is like a big sister to her son. Tami released her daughter to an older cousin who just happened to be looking for a baby to adopt. She now goes to school in a city near their home and visits the baby a couple times a month. She knows that her cousins are the baby's parents, and they have the say about everything in his life. But she gets the benefit of seeing him once in a while and knowing that she did what was best for all of them.

That solution might be a long shot in your case, but it wouldn't hurt to take a look at the family tree. I know one thing for sure, God has a plan for your baby's life, and he can make it happen.

Adoption isn't for everyone, but I think it's an option you should explore, especially if you know that you just can't raise a child right now. You might want to choose your baby's future parents from a list of people who really, really want a baby but can't get pregnant. Or you might already know someone who would love to raise your child. What a gift you have to give both the future parents and your child: the precious gift of life!

You can't go back in time and undo what is done; you can only move forward and do what you know in your heart to be right. It's a generous, selfless thing to carry a baby within you for nine months and then release him or her to someone else to raise. It won't be easy, but it is such a beautiful gift.

In Appendix A we cover some key questions about adoption, and an adoption agency or an adoption lawyer can give you more information. There are adoption counselors who will answer your questions without pressuring you into a decision. So *stand up*, be strong and do your homework.

KEY QUESTIONS:

Are your ideas about adoption based on emotion, or have you researched this option to discover the truth?

What are the pros and cons of adoption in your situation?

CHAPTER SEVEN

ABORTION

My name is Lisa, and a few years ago I wrote my own letter to Becky at the StandUpGirl Web site. Now I help her answer the hundreds of e-mails we get every week.

Like you, I had an unexpected pregnancy, but I didn't explore all the options you've looked at so far: keeping your baby and being a single mom, marrying your baby's father or releasing your child to a loving family for adoption. Maybe you're thinking, "None of those will work for me! There is no way I can have this baby!" That's exactly how I felt, so I chose what I thought would be the easiest route. I had an abortion.

Becky asked me to talk about abortion because I've been there. I guess the best way to start is to tell you my story.

LISA'S STORY

When I found out I was pregnant the first time, I was nineteen years old and living with my boyfriend. I worked in a hair salon as a hairdresser, just beginning my chosen career. I had always thought abortion was wrong, but my beliefs were based on what I'd been told. I'd never done any research on my own to find out what unborn babies were like or how they developed.

When my pregnancy test showed positive, I sat there in shock. My boyfriend was out of town, so when I quit shaking, I called him on his cell phone and just blurted it out: "I'm pregnant! I have to have an abortion. How can you not be here at a time like this?" It's amazing that he even understood me I was sobbing so hard. I needed someone to share this awful time with me, but there was no way he could come home. I felt so alone.

When he did get home three weeks later, my boyfriend didn't argue with me about the abortion; he just drove me to the abortion mill. I was shocked at how many girls were there! Some of them were so young, and they all looked sad and frightened. I cried so hard that I could hardly catch my breath, so they pulled me aside and took me to one of the head nurses. She watched me for a minute, then asked, "Are you sure you really want to do this?"

I could not honestly tell her yes, so I blurted out the truth. "My mom will kill me if she finds out, and I'm afraid because I've started doing some drugs." The nurse did not give me any positive options. She just nodded, said, "OK" and led me back into the other room.

Now I know that deep down inside I wanted someone to say, "You can have this baby, and everything will be OK." I needed someone to reach out to me, not just watch me do something that I would regret for the rest of my life. But after two hours of tests—urine samples, blood samples and so on—they put me on a gurney in a room with four other girls, separated only by a curtain hanging on silver rings from the ceiling. The nurse came in, examined me, said, "You're eleven weeks," and walked away.

What I didn't realize then, and what they did not tell me, was that at eleven weeks my baby had a heartbeat, little hands, little fingers and little toes. He sucked his thumb because that is pleasurable, and he also experienced pain.

When they rolled me out into the hallway, I was still crying. The abortionist leaned down and whispered in my ear, "Dear, if you continue to cry like this, you will hurt much more after the surgery." Though that doesn't seem very caring, it was the only kind touch that I remember during my experience. I nodded my head and bit my lip to hold back any more tears.

When they rolled me into the prep room, they put me next to a beautiful young girl. I remember looking over at her, and as she lay there a tear rolled back on her face. I had just enough time to wonder if she was as scared as I was, and then they took her away.

It seemed like only minutes later that they rolled me into a cold white room, put a mask on my face and told me to count backward from ten to one. When I woke up the physical and emotional pain nearly crushed me. I knew the baby was gone. I felt empty and horribly alone. I named him Vincent, and oh, how I wish I had him with me today.

About four years later I had my second abortion—my daughter, Alicia. That's right, even though the first experience was so traumatic, I did it again. I tried to cover the pain and the guilt with drugs and alcohol and further promiscuity. I felt angry too.

The abortions were the results of my own poor choices. Still, I have to think that if someone had been there to love me and pay attention to what I was going through, things might have worked out differently. No one explained what abortion was like or told me anything about fetal development. No one warned me how I might feel afterward, and at the time I was too scared to ask.

Please don't let that happen to you. Read the information in this book and others like it. I found out the hard way that abortion didn't make my babies "go away." Vincent and Alicia will always live in my heart. I still think about my babies and wonder what they would be like today if I had made different choices.

HOW IT'S DONE

OK, so you may still think that because of your circumstances, an abortion is your only option. Remember how we talked about knowing the facts before you decide? Well, here are the facts I wish someone had told me.

First of all, there are two main types of abortion: surgical and chemical. I had surgical abortions under a general anesthetic, which means they put me out and I didn't feel anything until it was over. Some insurance policies do not pay for a general anesthetic, especially if the woman is under fourteen weeks along, which is when most abortions are performed. Instead the abortionist uses a local anesthetic to numb the cervix so he can dilate it.

Earlier we talked about the hormone that causes the cervix to close up like a tight fist. A woman's body is programmed to keep the baby in the womb and keep infection out. To get inside the uterus, the abortionist has to dilate the cervix in one of two ways.

One way is to insert a series of metal rods, one at a time, each one slightly thicker than the last, until the cervix is open enough to allow the abortion tool in. Another way is to insert thin sticks of seaweed, called laminaria, several hours before the actual abortion. The sponge-like material absorbs body fluids and swells, opening the cervix.[1]

I know I sound as if I'm quoting from a textbook, but there's really no other way to explain this.

There are three kinds of surgical methods used to abort a baby under fourteen weeks' gestation. The first one is an MVA, or manual vacuum aspiration. The abortionist inserts into the uterus a syringe attached to some tubing and suctions the baby out. This method is used up to seven weeks after a woman's last period.

Sometimes an MVA is performed before a medical examination has proved the woman is pregnant. An MVA can be very dangerous. Even abortionists are leery of the method, because they may not get all of the tissue out, which could cause an infection or leave the woman still pregnant! Some doctors contend that this early abortion procedure is much more painful than a later abortion.

Another method is suction curettage. This is the most common procedure and is done anywhere from six to fourteen weeks after the first day of the woman's last period. The abortionist dilates the cervix, inserts some tubing and then connects it to a vacuum aspiration machine. The doctor can't see exactly where the baby is attached to the uterus, so he rotates the tubing around by feel. The force of the suction pulls apart the baby's body, tears the placenta from the uterine wall and then sucks it all out of the uterus. The suction is about twenty-five times stronger than that of a household vacuum.[2] The woman's body will shake, and there will be some pain. Still this procedure is considered to be the safest of all three surgical alternatives.

The third type of surgical abortion is a D and C, or dilation and curettage. This is also done six to fourteen weeks after the woman's last period. This method isn't used very often because it requires a general anesthetic. The cervix is dilated in the same way, but instead of a suction device, the abortionist uses a sharp, curved blade to cut the baby into parts and scrape the pieces along with the placenta out of the mother's body.[3] There is a risk that the blade might nick the wall of the uterus and cause heavy bleeding or infection. [4]

I'm honestly not trying to gross you out. If you're really thinking about having an abortion, I'd rather you know the truth now than be shocked by it later. I cried so hard when I discovered this information after I'd already gone through my abortions.

No matter which of these methods is used, there will be some pain and bleeding. The abortion staff gives the woman a little time to recover, then sends her home with instructions about the aftereffects. The bleeding is like a heavy period. It's possible with any method of abortion to have really heavy bleeding that can't be controlled or to develop an infection afterward. Death is rare in an early abortion, but hemorrhaging, increased pain or a fever signal an immediate trip to the emergency room.

With any surgical abortion there are risks of scarring and of tearing the cervix or uterus, which might make it hard for the woman to have a baby later. These physical problems happen in about one in a hundred early-term abortions.[5]

CHEMICAL ABORTIONS

When I had my two abortions, the chemical type was not available. Now a chemical abortion procedure known as RU-486 or mifepristone has been legalized in the United States, but it's still controversial because of its physical and emotional impact on women. A lot of doctors won't use it.[6]

Chemical abortion is used very early in a pregnancy—within four to seven weeks after a woman's last period. After a dose of the mifepristone, the woman is sent home. Mifepristone stops the embryo from staying attached to the uterus and stops the baby's growth. Two days later the woman goes back to the doctor's office or clinic and receives a dose of another medication called misprostol, which causes the uterus to contract and expel the baby.[7]

One problem with this type of abortion is that it doesn't always work. If the baby has not been expelled by the final checkup, a surgical abortion is performed.[8]

Another drug sometimes used is Methotrexate. Normally used to treat cancer, it kills the embryo cells by preventing their division. This drug is given by injection. Five to seven days later a dose of misprostol helps to expel the baby.[9]

The risks of chemical abortion include heavy bleeding, vomiting, diarrhea and death.[10] Here's one example from a newspaper article released by the Associated Press:

> *An abortion pill implicated in the death of an 18-year-old California woman last fall will add new warnings linking RU-486 to the risk of serious bacterial infection.*
>
> *Holly Patterson died Sept. 17, 2003, of septic shock caused by inflammation of the uterus. The teen died weeks after taking RU-486 to terminate an unplanned pregnancy....*
>
> *Mifeprex [a brand name for RU-486] already carries a black box warning, the [FDA] agency's most strident alert, to highlight other safety concerns. The FDA said that the drug's black box warning will expand, adding information about such rare but potentially life-threatening complications as serious bacterial infections and bleeding that can follow any abortion, including one induced by Mifeprex.*
>
> *Since the drug was approved, the agency has received reports of serious bacterial infection, bleeding, ectopic pregnancies that have ruptured and death.* [11]

It's really hard for me to talk about this. But I can't take the chance that you might miss these warnings and put yourself at risk.

EMOTIONAL CONSEQUENCES

The emotional risks of abortion are just as bad as the physical ones. We've had so many letters from women on this subject that it would be impossible to print them all here or on the Web site. Here are just a few:

Dear Becky,

To any girls out there who are thinking about having an abortion, please do your homework before you decide. Most of the girls I've talked to had the same reactions as I did. I hated myself for what I'd done and resented the people in my life who should have helped me but didn't. Abortion even drives some girls to commit suicide[12] because they can't live with the fact that they killed their own baby. Others end up pregnant six months later to have a "replacement" baby—even though no baby can be replaced.

No matter what the circumstances, abortion is a no-win situation. It's been several years since Stephanie's abortion, but she still suffers from hurt and confusion about her situation:

Dear Becky,

In 2001 I had an abortion. I've tried to "forget and forgive," but I just can't seem to get over it. The only one who even knew I was pregnant was my boyfriend. He said he'd be there to support me no matter what I decided. But then he said, "Steph, I'm not ready to be a father."

That stuck with me. I grew up without a father and often felt like half of me was missing. I didn't want to do that to a child.

At seven weeks along I started to do all the right things. I cut back on cigarettes and passed on the wine and beer. I added more milk and vegetables to my diet and bought a bottle of prenatal vitamins. But the whole time I knew what I was going to do.

I had the abortion at ten weeks along, in the hospital under anesthetic. After it was done, I knew right away that I was no longer pregnant, just empty and so sad. When my boyfriend went home that night, I felt so alone.

I still feel alone. It's been four years, and I still relive that day. I realize how angry I am at us. We are still together, we have good jobs and a nice home, but a part of me is missing that can never be replaced. I want so badly to have another baby and do the right thing this time. My boyfriend says he is still not ready to be a father, and I should be happy with all of the nice things we have. I take my birth control pills and cry every month when my period comes.

I guess the worst part is, I can't talk to anyone about this because no one knows! That's part of why I'm writing you. I needed to talk it out, but I also want to warn other girls like me to really think about the aftermath of an abortion. It can set off some drastic emotions, and they might not be able to handle it.

Stephanie

Boy, can I relate. After all these years I still grieve over my decision and the loss of my babies.

Stephanie is in a hard place, torn between love for the baby she lost and love for the man she is with. It's my prayer that she will come to a place where she can forgive herself and her partner. It's not an easy road to travel, but there is help out there.

Becky and I gave Stephanie some suggestions, which we include at the end of this chapter. There are also resources in Appendix B, under "Abortion Information and Post-Abortion Help," that might be helpful to you if you are regretting an abortion.

A SECOND-TRIMESTER ABORTION

The methods I've told you about are done during the first trimester only. In the second trimester—over fourteen weeks pregnant—the methods are much more difficult and very painful for the baby. Such was Sandi's experience:

> *Dear Becky,*
>
> *My husband and I had been happily married for two years when we discovered I was pregnant. We were overjoyed! We had good jobs and a nice home. We weren't rich, but it didn't matter; we were more than ready to start a family.*
>
> *But then it all went horribly wrong.*
>
> *For years I had suffered from bouts of mild depression, but it was something we'd learned to live with. Now that I was pregnant, it seemed to get worse. I had to quit my job because all I could do was cry. The doctor said that medication for depression would hurt the baby. We decided that it would be good for me to just stay home and take care of myself. The hormones would calm down*

once the baby was a little further along, and I'd be just fine.

But that didn't happen.

At sixteen weeks along I felt so bad that I made a snap decision to have an abortion. My husband cried but agreed. He said he just wanted me to be normal again, and maybe if I wasn't pregnant, I could get some medication and we could try again when I was well.

Neither of us realized how long the process would take or how horrible it would be. It took almost a month before I could get in to see a doctor. He examined me and asked why I wanted an abortion at this late date. I told him I was too depressed to carry on with the pregnancy. He patted my shoulder and gave me the name of a doctor who might consider performing a late-term abortion.

By the time I was able to get an appointment at that clinic, I was seven months along and not thinking straight at all. They handed me a pamphlet of information about the procedure, but my hands were shaking so badly, my husband had to read it to me. He was repulsed by what he read, but I didn't really understand a word of it. I was so upset, and he was so desperate to have a normal wife, we agreed to go ahead with it.

That next week was awful. I got drunk every day to numb the emotional pain. He worked overtime as much as he could to get away from the

*turmoil at home. When the time came we drove to
the abortion clinic in silence.*

*The nurse scanned my intake papers and
asked, "Are you sure about this?"*

*"No." I felt as if I had yelled for the world to
hear, but in reality it was only a whisper from
within my heart.*

*I asked if I would feel any pain. She told me
some women feel nothing and remember nothing,
but most of the time the woman feels a little pain.
I wondered if the baby would feel it too.*

*They used rods to dilate my cervix and several
hours later gave me some pills. It seemed like
forever, as I suffered from sharp abdominal pain
and heavy bleeding. I kept asking, "Is my baby
dead yet?" No one answered.*

*Finally, as they wheeled me away from my
husband toward the operating room, I realized
that I didn't want to kill my baby. But by then it
was too late.*

*The operation itself was awful. First they
broke my water, then they used an abortion
instrument to pull my twenty-three-week-old baby
apart and rip him, piece by piece, out of my body.
I hoped my baby couldn't feel the pain I felt. I
know now that he did.*

*Nothing will ever be the same. Instead of
"getting well" I am more depressed than ever and
feel so guilty about what I have done. I love my
husband but have asked him to move out for a*

while. I am as angry with him as I am with myself. How could we have done such a terrible thing? Why didn't he step in for me and make the doctors treat my depression? Why did he allow me to go through such a horrible thing?

I hate those doctors and I hate myself. There is no way anything will ever be the same for me again. Abortion is wrong. There is nothing I can do to make up for what I did. If there is any hope for us, I can't see it right now.

Thanks for reading this. At least it helped some to write it all down.

Sandi

GETTING HELP

Becky and I both cried when we read Sandi's letter. It must have been so hard for her to write, but she was wise to get her feelings out. She needs to deal with her anger and grieve the loss of her child. Most of all, she needs to realize that there is hope for her and for her husband.

I learned that anger and bitterness toward others only hurt me more. I needed to learn to forgive, but I didn't know how to do that alone. Then I met someone who changed my life. I didn't even realize he'd been there all along. He had loved me through all of it: the abortions, the drinking, the drugs and the sex. He showed me love and forgiveness, even though I didn't deserve it.

His name is Jesus Christ. He died and rose again so I could be free from my sin. He took away my shame and sorrow. He paid the price that allows me to have a relationship with God. I am finally free.

What Jesus gave me I want to share with every woman who has had the horrible experience of abortion. Whether you know it or not, he loves you too and wants to show you his mercy. If you want to know more, please go to StandUpGirl.com and e-mail me. I would love to help you.

If you already suffer from depression, as Sandi did even before her abortion, I urge you to find a doctor who understands depression and can help you through it now. There are many new medications that can help restore the balance of hormones in your body. Chronic depression is nothing to be ashamed of; it's a dangerous disorder that requires medical care.

Look in the phone book under "mental health." Call a clinic or doctor's office and ask for a consultation appointment. Ask someone to *stand up* and go to the first visit with you. Make sure the person you see is someone you can trust. There is help for you, but you can't do it alone.

Becky advised Sandi to get medical help, then continued:

I lost a baby through miscarriage, so I understand some of your anger and pain. It takes time to get over such a significant loss. Be patient with yourself. Sometimes it helps to name your baby. Have you done that yet?

It will take time to forgive yourself, your loved ones and the doctors who did not listen. But there is help out there. Find another doctor and reach out to God. He will bring you the healing and forgiveness that you so desperately seek.

We were able to direct Sandi to a counselor who helped restore her faith in herself, her husband and her God. This help is available to you. Consult Appendix B for information about post-abortion help. And be sure to read the next chapter, in which we talk about the grief process in more detail.

LATE REGRETS
One final letter speaks for itself:

> *Dear Lisa,*
>
> *I was eighteen years old and six weeks pregnant when I had an abortion. I am thirty-nine now, married and the mother of a beautiful baby boy.*
>
> *When I was pregnant with this little son, I remember thinking that he was inside me, growing, feeling warm and loved, knowing that I would protect him and keep him safe. That was when the terrible guilt and regret about the abortion really began to haunt me.*
>
> *If I had known then what I know now, I would never have gone through with it. But I cannot undo what I did. It is not something that "happened to me" or something that "I went through." Afraid and ashamed of being pregnant, I chose what I thought was the easy way out. I really believed that it was a quick "procedure" and that, afterward, my life would go on as if I had never gotten pregnant. Wrong!*
>
> *Now, as I hold my little son, it has really hit home that a pregnancy is a baby, not a blob of tissue, and an abortion is not a "procedure" or a*

"quick medical visit." It is killing the baby.

I never realized the emotional problems women face later in their lives. No matter how far along you were, it's hard to swallow the truth that you killed your child.

I remember over the years confiding to others that I had an abortion. I know now that I was looking for forgiveness from someone because I knew I had done something wrong.

Part of my decision to have an abortion came from relying on my emotions, which I know now were partially fueled by hormones. I felt, "Well, if I am this upset and scared, then I must not want this baby." No one ever mentioned the power of hormones to me at the abortion clinic. No one told me that pregnancy was not just about me. It was about the baby I carried and that baby's future. It was my job as a mother to protect my child.

If I had chosen to stand up and take responsibility for my situation instead of giving in to fear, I would have a sense of pride knowing that I gave my child life. I share my story in the hope that it might prevent even one woman from making the same mistake I made. Stand up girl! The rest of your life and your baby's life depend on it!

Lori

KEY QUESTIONS:

What are the pros and cons of abortion?

If you are grieving an abortion, what can you do to get help?

CHAPTER EIGHT

LOSS AND GRIEF

I've received thousands of letters from women of all ages about their pregnancies, and every one of them expresses fear or sadness over some type of loss. Any pregnancy, planned or not, brings with it loss.

Of course, a pregnancy carried to term also brings obvious gain. You have, with your partner, produced a new life to nurture and love. Maternal instinct can be overwhelming. If your pregnancy is a surprise, those positive feelings may be hidden beneath the uncertainty and fear, but the joy and excitement of new life are almost always there.

Lisa says, "I can't believe the joy our little daughter has brought to our lives. It's brought our whole family closer. My husband and I had no choice; we had to grow up. We planned for our baby but were still in for some surprises. The most difficult loss we experienced was a good night's sleep!"

CONFRONTING THE LOSS

OK, a good night's sleep may seem like a small loss to someone who did not expect to have a baby at all. Yet it's good to realize that even the couple who *plans* for a baby well ahead of time will experience loss: loss of freedom to go and do as they please; maybe a loss of income if the wife must leave her job. Yes, their lives will change.

The changes in your life may mean major loss. As you saw from the letters in previous chapters, loss can include everything from no high school diploma to an interrupted career. Some girls lose their parents' respect, and many even lose their homes. Many of them lose the baby's father. Others marry the boyfriend before either of them is ready and, instead of longed-for independence, acquire responsibility for another human life.

No matter who we are or what our circumstances are, life includes loss. At any moment we could lose our health, our freedom or someone we love. Pregnancy just makes us that much more vulnerable.

Abortion brings with it the greatest loss imaginable, because sooner or later the parents realize that their child died by their choice. If you have had an abortion, you could experience emotional symptoms now or years down the road. In order to heal you might need medical or psychological help. A private counselor or a post-abortion support group can help. Appendix B can direct you to some good resources. There *is* help for you.

Adoption also brings with it a huge sense of loss. You have chosen to give this baby life, made the sacrifices necessary to nurture him or her for nine months, suffered through labor and delivery, then handed your precious baby over to another family to raise. No matter how well thought out or how positive you are that this is the right decision, you still are losing a part of yourself, and you will grieve.

MISCARRIAGE

Most pregnancies move along without much difficulty. The baby is born somewhere around the prospective due date, healthy and whole. There are the exceptions to this natural progression of events, and it's these exceptions that rock our world.

When something goes wrong and your baby does not survive, you probably want to know why. Did you do something wrong? Was the baby deformed or incurably ill? The truth is, there is not always an answer to the *why* of miscarriage. But whatever the circumstances, the loss of a baby brings grief.

Linda's second pregnancy resulted in a miscarriage at barely four weeks along. She felt sick and dizzy, passed what looked like a large blood clot, then bled for several days.

> *It felt like a heavy period. I went to bed for a day or two, then felt better except for this weird sense of loss. Sure, I wasn't that far along, but I couldn't help wondering if that baby was a boy or a girl. What would he or she have looked like?*
>
> *I went on to have another boy, and I still like to think that the baby I lost was a girl. That happened over thirty years ago, but the thought that I have a third child waiting for me in heaven still moves me to excitement and tears. I can't wait to hold her!*

Most miscarriages happen in the first trimester of pregnancy. This seems like the easiest time to lose a baby, but the grief can still be intense.

I was only eight weeks along with another child when I had some heavy bleeding. When the doctor checked me out, he couldn't find the baby's heartbeat, so he sent me in for an ultrasound.

As soon as I saw the ultrasound screen, I knew something was wrong. The nurse shook her head. "I'm so sorry," she said, "but this isn't a normal pregnancy. You won't be able to carry it through."

I felt as if someone had punched me in the stomach. Our baby was dead. I would never be able to hold him or her. I cried and cried. I knew I hadn't been feeling "right," but I never expected this.

The obstetrician explained that I had a very rare molar pregnancy. This type of pregnancy results from chromosomal issues early on. As it does not normally terminate on its own and can be dangerous to a mother if carried too long, he said he would have to do a D and C. At that time I associated a D and C with abortion! How could God let this happen to me?

To make matters worse, I had to check into the maternity ward where I had delivered my first child, Joy, and then I became sick from the anesthetic. I recovered from that the next day, but the emotional pain was another story. I thought I would go crazy. Wanting to be alone, I refused to talk to anyone.

I can honestly say that I had never grieved like that before. Others took care of my family and brought meals, while I used my time alone to think and pray. I had to ask God to take away the fear and pain.

Our whole family needed healing and peace. Little Joy

kept patting my tummy as if the baby were still there. She didn't understand at all. I know I will see the baby I lost in heaven someday, but I still think of the little one with sadness and pain in my heart.

LATER LOSS
Late miscarriage and death at birth are even more devastating. Peg's baby died in the womb at eight months and was born two weeks later. The family held a private service and buried their little girl. Carrie Ann never experienced life on earth, and her parents' grief was deep and real.

Maggie and Rob knew their baby would not live outside the womb. The doctors clearly explained the inoperable problems that would kill their son the minute he was born. They chose to carry him to term because they believe only God can make the decision for life or death. They received professional counseling to help them overcome their feelings of despair.

Ray and Tina nearly sustained a double loss. Their baby was five months along when the doctors diagnosed multiple, untreatable birth defects. They told the couple there was no doubt the baby would die before birth or immediately after, and there was a very real danger that Tina could die as well.

Ray felt trapped with an impossible decision: Should he allow them to take his baby's life or risk losing his wife? For him the choice was devastating but obvious. They could have other children, but he could not risk losing his wife.

Tina took a different stance. She would not abort their baby under any circumstances. The baby's life belonged to

God, as did her own, and she felt strongly that it was not her decision to make.

Talk about a crisis pregnancy! Ray could not take the pressure. He was ready to move out, but his friends and family rallied around him and helped him hold it together. When the time came, baby Jen was born. Her little body looked perfect, but internally she had many defects. The doctors confirmed that there was no way she would survive for very long.

The doctors were amazed, however, that Tina's labor was short, the delivery easy and her physical recovery fast. She never once came close to death.

Ray, Tina and other family members took turns holding Jen around the clock. She could not eat, yet she didn't cry. Each person who held her reported an overwhelming feeling of peace as the baby looked up at him or her with serene blue eyes. They all said later that the baby smiled at them, but they didn't want to say anything because a baby that age is not supposed to smile!

Baby Jen lived long enough to bring peace and blessings to every member of her immediate family. After eighteen hours she slipped quietly into Jesus' arms. I don't know about you, but that gives me goose bumps.

FACING GRIEF

No matter what type of loss you experience in your pregnancy, it brings a mental and emotional response that we call grief. Grief can creep into your life, like fog in a forest, or strike like a hammer blow and knock you to your knees. If you admit your grief and allow yourself to go through its process, you will heal faster than if you bury it inside and go along as if nothing has happened.

With that in mind, I would like to share with you the process of grief and how, with help, you can get through it. Grieving is a painful process. It involves emotional turmoil, depression, anger, helplessness, rage, loneliness, resentment and hopelessness. It can cause physical symptoms such as eating disorders, sleep disturbances, sexual dysfunction, physical illness and pain, as well as family and marital problems. There are six major steps to the grieving process.[1]

S h o c k

Shock can sometimes be a blessing, especially when dealing with an unexpected death. It numbs our emotions enough to allow us to function when there are decisions to make and gives us time to gather a support system to help us through the grieving process. Friends, family and certainly your pastor and physician should be part of the team.

D e n i a l

Our mind refuses to believe the loss has happened, especially if it is as final as death. Hopefully the denial stage is short. For if we bury our grief and refuse to face the truth, we just postpone the pain and make it worse.

A n g e r

"How could God do this to me?" "How could my partner leave me?" "My parents had no right to kick me out." "Why did my baby have to die?" "How could I have made such a stupid choice?" All of these questions and more may run through your mind.

Anger is a normal part of the grieving process. But if you get stuck in this stage and are unable to move forward, anger can lead to bitterness and a desire for revenge that will plague you and make your life even more miserable.

Bargaining

Many people will bargain with God, even those who don't believe in him. "God, if you will do...for me, I will do...for you." Or, "Billy, if you come back to me, I will do whatever you want." Bargaining is a natural reaction to loss. We are helpless to change our circumstances, and for a time we feel that someone or something else might be able to reverse the situation.

Depression

To one extent or another depression is always part of the grieving process. We feel sad and perhaps even cry all the time. We are sure life will never be the same, and we wonder how or if we can ever go on. The smallest decision evades our brain cells, and a suggested activity causes us to run for cover. We either sleep all the time or can't sleep at all. We feel irritable and lonely, restless and afraid. Life basically sucks, and we don't want to do this anymore.

Depression is probably the most dangerous stage of grief and the easiest in which to get stuck. We almost always need help to work our way out of this one. Remember the support system we talked about? Well, if ever you needed those people, you need them now!

As with everything else we're dealing with in this book, you can manage grief if you are educated on the subject and plan ahead of time how you will deal with it.

That doesn't come naturally. But then neither do the decisions you have to make about your pregnancy.

Whatever you do, please don't try to go through this alone. Gather the troops, tell them what to look for and ask for help. Get help from your doctor, psychologist or a professional counselor. If you are too far down to make the appointment yourself, have a friend make it for you and, if necessary, drive you there!

Acceptance

When all is said and done, acceptance should be the final stage of grief. That doesn't mean the end of all pain or loneliness. It does mean that you realize the past is over and you are able to go on with your life.

Forgiveness

Yes, I know that forgiveness is not formally one of the six major stages of grief, but I also know from experience that until we can forgive ourselves and others involved in our crisis situation, we can have no peace.

In the Bible Jesus says, "Forgive, and you will be forgiven" (Luke 6:37). How did God forgive us? He sent his only Son to die on the cross as the penalty for every sin you and I have ever committed. This was his gift to us; we did nothing to earn it. That's what grace is: a gift we receive even though we don't deserve it. If we accept God's gift of forgiveness and love, we will spend eternity with him.

If we ignore God's forgiveness, refuse his gift and refuse to forgive others who have hurt us, our life on earth and beyond the grave will be spent separated from the very one who conquered death and promised life. To me that is a scary prospect.

Forgiveness is a choice each one of us can make. My prayer for you is that you will *stand up* and receive God's gift.

KEY QUESTIONS:
What is the nature of your loss?

At what stage are you in the grieving process?

Where can you find help to move on?

PART THREE

FACING PREGNANCY

CHAPTER NINE

YOUR BABY

Time out! I don't know about you, but I need a break. We've talked a lot about how to manage the crisis of an unexpected pregnancy, and we've talked about all of your options. Maybe you still aren't sure what you're going to do, but let's stop for a few minutes and look at the good stuff.

The way a baby develops in the womb is awesome. The way those tiny cells are formed into one unique human being can only be called a miracle. Another miracle is that we can now actually see pictures—even 3-D pictures—of the baby growing inside us. In this book we can show you some beautiful drawings, so come with me on one of the most awesome journeys you'll ever take: a tour of how your baby grows in your womb.

By the time you've missed a period, taken a pregnancy test and discovered that, yes, it is positive and, yes, you are pregnant, that tiny fertilized egg is already twenty-one to twenty-eight days old. This miniature, rapidly developing human being has already nestled into the lining of your uterus and is drawing nourishment from your body.

At *eighteen to twenty-one days* the baby's heart begins to beat. The foundations of the brain, spinal cord and nervous system are laid. Arms, legs, eyes and ears have also begun to show. The backbone and muscles are forming.[1]

At *thirty days* the baby has already grown ten thousand times its original size to a quarter inch long. Blood flows in the baby's veins but stays separate from your blood, because the placenta forms a unique barrier that gives the baby a separate circulatory system but still allows it to take food and oxygen from your body. I don't know about you, but I find that totally amazing!

At *five weeks* your baby looks like a little tadpole, shrimp or peanut. But as you can see by the drawing, he or she is absolutely a human baby. These early pictures always make me smile. Can you see the fingers on the baby's tiny hand? And the eyes are now dark with color. The brain has already started to develop, and somewhere in that fifth week brain waves can actually be recorded.

By the time the baby is *six weeks* old, you've probably missed your second period and are ready to make those hard choices we've already talked about. Meanwhile, the baby continues to grow. The liver now takes over and produces blood cells, and the brain controls movement of muscles and internal organs.

Week seven is a busy one for the baby. He or she can move around, though you cannot yet feel the movement. The jaw takes shape, including tiny teeth buds in the gums. If you could study the baby's face and head you could say, "I think he has ears like Uncle John's!"

The baby's eyes are so sensitive to light—yes, even in your womb—that the eyelids seal shut and then reopen when the baby is about seven months along. The baby now looks like a tiny alien swimming in a bubble of amniotic fluid, which among other things protects the growing baby from the bumps and jolts of your everyday life. She or he even swallows some of the fluid, which might cause hiccups. Don't worry; you won't feel them yet.

You are carrying another person in your body!

I'll never forget the day this became real to me. I had a job walking a friend's dog. He was a good-sized Labrador retriever and could pull me along pretty fast. Sometimes it was a question of who was walking whom! Anyway, he took off after a bird or a squirrel or something. I wasn't paying attention, and he pulled me right off my feet. I landed hard, face down on the sidewalk.

Thank God, I wasn't seriously hurt, and neither was my baby. But I realized, "Wow, I'd better be more careful. I'm carrying around this tiny human being, and I'm responsible for her!" I knew it wasn't just about me anymore. It was about me and the precious little one I carried inside.

At *eight weeks*, or about two months of age, your baby is about an inch long. He or she would fit in a nutshell, but everything is there: hands, feet, head, organs, brain, everything needed for a national identity card! Even the baby's fingerprints will show up in another few days.[2] A baby this age is called a fetus. *Fetus* is the Latin word for "young one" or "offspring."[3]

If you could touch your baby, he or she would feel your touch and respond by moving. Yes, the baby *can* feel both pleasure and pain. The stomach produces digestive juices, the kidneys begin to function, and taste buds are just beginning to form.

One of my most incredible experiences was when I went to the doctor for my eight-week checkup. The doctor placed a special stethoscope on my abdomen. At first I heard a slow, rhythmic "bom...bom."

"That's your own heartbeat and the pulse of your placenta," the doctor said.

He moved the stethoscope slowly over my abdomen. All of a sudden I heard a faster beat, like the flutter of bird wings. The doctor smiled. "That's your baby's heart."

I was completely mesmerized by the sound. My baby's heart, beating so strong! From that moment on everything seemed so much more real.

Have you ever held a newborn and had her curve those little fingers around one of yours? It's an awesome experience, but what you might not realize is that at about *nine weeks* along your baby can already do that.

By *ten weeks* you may see a little bulge in your stomach. That's because your uterus has doubled in size. Things are moving right along! Your baby squints and swallows and can wrinkle the forehead and frown.

By *eleven weeks* the baby is about two inches long. The shrimp appearance has vanished, and he or she looks like a miniature newborn. The muscle movements become more coordinated. The baby urinates, makes complex facial expressions and even smiles.[4]

At *twelve weeks*, or three months along, the baby sleeps, awakens and exercises muscles energetically. He kicks and turns his feet, curls and spreads his toes.

He can move his thumbs and bend his wrists. He opens and closes his mouth, presses his lips together and would make a tight fist if you could stroke his palm. He even practices breathing the amniotic fluid to help develop the respiratory system.

At *thirteen weeks* her face is prettier and her movements more graceful. Her head is covered with hair as fine as peach fuzz. If you could study her facial expressions, you might say, "She has my smile, my nose and her father's chin, but her ears still look like Uncle John's!" The baby now has vocal cords but, as the womb is without air, cannot cry. The sex organs are now apparent, but it will be a few weeks until you can tell for sure if you have a boy or a girl.[5]

By end of the *fourth month* most, if not all, of the unpleasant pregnancy symptoms should be gone. The baby moves around a lot, and you should be able to feel that movement any day now.

When I think about the first four months of a baby's life, I get goose bumps. God's design for human growth is so fast! Your baby is now eight to ten inches long and weighs over half a pound. The umbilical cord, attached to the baby's belly at one end and your uterus at the other, transports three hundred quarts of fluid a day. It delivers nourishment and takes away waste at the rate of a round-trip every thirty seconds.

I was sitting in my history class when I felt that first flutter—just a tiny movement inside my belly, unlike anything I'd ever felt before. I wanted to stand up and shout,

"My baby moved!" Over the following weeks I found my hands constantly drawn to my stomach. I cradled the tiny bump, talked to her and stroked her through my belly.

If you haven't talked or sung to your baby, now is a good time to start. The ears are functioning, and your baby can hear your voice, your heartbeat and even noises from outside your body.

By the beginning of your *fifth month* your baby is about twelve inches long, and half your pregnancy is over. When I got to that stage, I was both excited and relieved. I felt confident I would carry to term. I knew my baby was fully developed and just needed to grow.

But it was all still such a mystery. What would my baby look like? What kind of personality would she have?

TAKE A LOOK INSIDE

When Keith and I went in for my ultrasound, the evidence of a real baby inside me thrilled me to my toes. The technician put some sticky gel on my belly and ran the scanner over my skin. The monitor screen showed a little moving form. The technician pointed out my baby's body, her arms and legs, fingers and toes. She was kicking around and seemed to be having a great time!

When we zeroed in on her head and face, we could see her features so clearly. Beautiful, awesome, amazing! We stared spellbound as she lifted her tiny hand as if to wave. My throat tightened up, and Keith and I looked at each other with tears streaming down our faces.

Here's what some other women have to say about their ultrasound experiences:

I had an ultrasound today. I saw and felt him move and heard his heart beat. I can't get over the fact that a real baby, my baby, is moving inside me!

...

When I found out I was pregnant, I didn't want the baby. Then I had an ultrasound. When I saw her rolling around inside me and heard her heartbeat, she became real to me. She wasn't just a "thing" anymore. After that I knew, no matter what happened, I would have my baby.

A while back I got a letter from a girl who had been the victim of a brutal rape that resulted in a pregnancy. She lost the baby and was told by her doctors that she could never have another child. A few years later she got married. Their living situation was bad, and when she found out she was pregnant again, she had to quit her job. She and her husband were scared to death. They couldn't afford a baby, and she would probably miscarry anyway, so they decided to have an abortion.

They sought information from an abortion clinic and a crisis pregnancy center. When they saw the pictures of unborn babies—much like the ones in this chapter—and read the facts about abortion, they hesitated. But they were still scared and made the appointment for the abortion.

The day before the scheduled abortion, they went back to the pregnancy clinic for an ultrasound. I'll let her tell you the rest in her own words.

> *When we saw our healthy fourteen-week-old baby*
> *moving around inside me, all thoughts of*
> *abortion were gone. The nurse gave us prints of*
> *the ultrasound, and when we got home my*
> *husband studied them for the longest time, then*
> *grinned at me and said, "You cancel the*
> *appointment and I'll find a job, because we are*
> *having a baby!"*

This couple sought information about their baby, which is exactly what you did when you picked up this book. I hope you will come to the same decision this father did.

REACHING OUT

You may have seen the picture of Baby Sam, published in newspapers a few years ago. The unborn baby is twenty-one-week-old Samuel Alexander Armas, who is being operated on by surgeon Joseph Bruner. The picture shows an exposed uterus with the fingers of a tiny hand curved around the surgeon's finger.

Sam had been diagnosed with spina bifida, a disabling spinal condition. His parents were told that at least half of the unborn babies diagnosed with this problem are aborted. But Julie and Alex Armas did not consider abortion an option. "This was the baby God chose to give us," Alex said. "In our minds this was not a fifteen-week-old fetus but rather our new son, Samuel."

Baby Samuel's mother was an obstetrics nurse and knew of Dr. Bruner's remarkable surgical procedures. He performs these special operations while the baby is still in the womb. The doctor removes the uterus via c-section and makes a small incision in it so he can operate on the baby.

As Dr. Bruner completed the surgery on Samuel, the little guy reached his tiny but fully developed hand through the incision and firmly grasped the surgeon's finger. Dr. Bruner said that it was the most emotional moment of his life. For an instant he just froze. The photograph captures this amazing event with perfect clarity. The picture has been titled "Hand of Hope."

When Samuel's mother saw the photograph, she wept. She told the press, "This photo reminds us pregnancy isn't about disability or an illness, it's about a little person."[6]

Baby Samuel was born on time, in perfect health, the operation 100 percent successful. Is that awesome or what?

LIFE AND MORE LIFE

As my pregnancy progressed, it was so exciting to have my daughter move, as I could see it from the outside. I didn't even mind the kicks and jabs of feet and elbows and knees. Sometimes, when I lay on my back, she really put on a show—something between somersaults and a roller coaster ride. She would jump at a loud noise or go quiet when I played soft music. I knew she could feel the vibrations when I patted my belly.

When she pushed on my ribcage or bladder, I tried to shift her to a different position. Sometimes she moved, but only when she was good and ready! Even in the womb babies can have a mind of their own!

Six months is a real milestone. The baby grows eyebrows and eyelashes. He or she weighs about one and a half pounds. The baby's skin is so delicate it needs protection from the fluid around it, so it develops a special covering called vernix. If your baby were born at six months along and given the right medical care, he or she could survive.

When Marlene and Jim's first son was just twenty-one weeks along, Marlene started bleeding from her womb. An ultrasound didn't show much, but the baby seemed determined to be born. The couple was told that their baby would not survive if born that early, and the doctors didn't hold out much hope.

Unwilling to just give up and let their son die, Marlene and Jim decided to do everything possible to keep the baby in her womb. She spent days in the hospital on total bed rest and took drugs designed to delay her labor.

In spite of everything they tried, Marlene went into full labor at twenty-four weeks along. After twelve hours of hard contractions, baby John was born. He weighed exactly one pound, five ounces. The medical staff, certain that the child would not survive, encouraged the parents to just let him die.

The entire family refused. Baby John was put in neonatal care, then flown to a pediatric hospital, where he would receive special treatment for his under-developed lungs and eyes. He is now eight years old. Other than thick glasses to help with his damaged eyesight, he is a normal, intelligent, fun-loving little boy.

What if Marlene and Jim had taken the doctor's advice and allowed their little boy to die? That thought gives me the creeps.

THE HOME STRETCH!

If little John had stayed in the womb only a few more

weeks, he possibly would have good eyesight as well. At *seven months* the baby
opens and closes his eyes and looks
around.[7] Your baby also can hear, taste,
touch and best of all, recognize your
voice! The baby knows when mommy's
talking and, I'm sure, listens. Just watch the
reaction when you cuddle and talk to your baby
after birth.

By now, when your baby gets the hiccups, you will feel
it. My friend Linda used to dread her baby's hiccups
because she invariably got them too!

At *eight months* the baby's weight is
increasing rapidly and will continue to do so
until birth. The womb gets a little cramped, and
the baby can't move as freely as before. You will
feel the pressure as the baby stretches and turns,
then finally pushes into a head-down position that
signals he or she is ready to get out of there!

Toward the end of the *ninth month* the baby is ready
for birth. Most babies are born somewhere between 266
and 294 days. Typically he or she should weigh anywhere from six to nine pounds, but some come
really small and some really big. Your doctor will
probably give you a prediction of the baby's size,
but don't count on its accuracy!

Well, now that you know about what's
happening with your baby, you might want to
read the next chapter about what's happening
with you during these nine months.

KEY QUESTIONS:

What have you learned about the stages of your baby's development?

How far along is your baby right now?

What do you think about the picture of a baby at this stage?

CHAPTER TEN

YOUR BODY

I'm sure I already told you how I felt when my period was late. I had cramps, my breasts were sore, and I felt really bloated, just as if I were going to start any day. That's what kept me in denial.

But morning sickness and feeling grouchy weren't part of the normal picture, not to mention that my breasts had never been that big! That's what clued me in that this wasn't just a late period. As much as I wanted to be wrong, my body was telling me in no uncertain terms that I was pregnant.

Between vomiting and having to urinate, I felt as if I lived in the bathroom those first few weeks. I felt so tired, it was all I could do to get out of bed and drag myself to class. It didn't take long for me to realize that I could no longer work at night and go to school during the day.

You may or may not have all of these symptoms. If your symptoms are mild, count your blessings. If your symptoms are severe, you can be encouraged by the fact that they should go away after a while. Your body is making hormones that are needed for your baby to grow, and your system has to get used to them.

Every once in a while someone tells me, "I was sick the whole nine months!" If you're one of those few, take heart. Modern medicine can help make your pregnancy a lot more comfortable. But you do have to do your part.

TAKING CARE OF TWO

Your baby and your body are inseparable right now. Yes, you have separate circulatory systems, but the baby still gets nourishment from you. One of the first things I learned about prenatal care was "What goes into your body goes into your baby!" That's why it's so important to pay attention to your own health as soon as you know you're pregnant.

If you smoke, drink or take drugs, quit right away! Even cold medicine and aspirin can spell trouble for your baby. Your doctor can help you with any addictions you might have. I'm not saying it will be easy, but believe me, you and your baby will feel a whole lot better for it.

The key is to make these changes as soon as you know you are pregnant. If you take another look at chapter nine and see how your baby is developing right now, you'll understand how devastating these habits and medications can be to your baby's body.

As soon as you know you are pregnant, it would be a good idea to get some prenatal vitamins, either from the pharmacy or the doctor. There are good ones that don't require a prescription, but check the label to be sure they contain folic acid. Folic acid is a B vitamin that helps reduce the risk of birth defects of the brain and spinal cord. If you have questions about the vitamins you choose, ask the pharmacist or your doctor for advice.

We'll cover a lot of information in this chapter, but I would really recommend you take a prenatal class at a pregnancy clinic, hospital or community center. The pregnancy center where my friend works offers an eight-week course, just one hour a week, that covers everything from nutrition to breast-feeding, labor and delivery and newborn care.

There are many free centers like this throughout the country. (To find one in your area, call Care Net, 800-395-HELP.) These caring people—many of them volunteers—answer questions, offer pamphlets and books and are basically just there for you throughout your pregnancy. Centers often provide maternity and baby clothes and other items you'll need.

There are other resources listed in Appendix B of this book. The important thing is to have a safe, healthy and enjoyable pregnancy. And that is not as hard as you might think.

Before the end of the second month you should have your first prenatal checkup. The doctor or midwife you've chosen will examine you to be sure you are really pregnant. If you're not already on prenatal vitamins, she or he can suggest an over-the-counter brand or write you a prescription.

Go to this visit prepared with any questions you have about your baby or your own body. For instance, my friend Nola smoked cigarettes. She knew that smoking would harm her baby, but she was under a lot of stress and didn't think she'd be able to quit. Once she confided in her doctor, she was surprised at how much he was able to help. Following his instructions, she was able to cut back on cigarettes right away and quit altogether in just a few weeks. (We walked together and drank lots of orange juice. I'm proud of her, especially because she's stayed smoke-free for over two years.)

Jenny wrote to me because she'd been on birth control pills for months and drank several beers at a party the weekend before she found out she was pregnant. (Yes, she got pregnant even though she was on the pill. As you may know, abstinence is the only form of birth control that is 100 percent effective.) Jenny was afraid her baby would be retarded or deformed because of the pills and beer. I suggested she talk to her doctor. He was able to set her mind at ease, while cautioning her to discontinue use of both the pills and the alcohol for the duration of her pregnancy.

So if you need help with lifestyle changes, now is the time to ask for it. Your doctor will keep these things confidential and work with you to help you have a healthy pregnancy. That's what the doctor is there for.

EATING RIGHT

Eating right is easy once you get past the nausea stage. I obtained a chart from the pregnancy center that showed the five major food groups and how much of each type of food I should eat per day. At first I felt that it was way too much. But once my baby started growing, I could eat everything in sight!

Besides vitamins and the right balance of healthy food, it's really important to drink six to eight glasses of water, juice or milk a day. Milk is especially important. Women need extra calcium anyway, but when you're pregnant your body is building baby bones as well as strengthening your own. So if you wrinkle your nose at the sight of a glass of milk, check out your food group chart for some other good sources of calcium. You'd be surprised at how many choices you have.

When I was *three months* along I started to grow out of my clothes. I was back at school by then, and nobody there knew I was pregnant, so I left the top button of my jeans undone and wore baggy sweaters to cover the small bump in my stomach. Pants or skirts with an elastic waist work great, and you can top them with an oversized shirt or blouse.

I have to admit that I was really frustrated when my body changed shape and I started to gain weight. I didn't want to get fat and have to wear maternity clothes. My emotions were constantly in stress mode. I would look in the mirror, hold up my favorite outfits and have a real pity party. "I'll never fit into these clothes again!" I felt doomed to a future of huge ugly clothes, mounds of fat and disfiguring stretch marks.

About *four months* into my pregnancy, something incredible happened. I quit throwing up, and food smelled and tasted good again. I even began to crave certain foods. I remember begging Keith to go out and get me a bag of Zesty Cheese Doritos! My friend Linda craved chocolate malts. And a friend of hers wanted tacos for breakfast, lunch and dinner. We ate right most of the time, but once in a while…

I found I had much more energy and was able to go back to some of the activities I had enjoyed before pregnancy—like shopping! When I was out looking for a bigger bra, I found some really cute maternity clothes at a thrift shop. But there were lots of times when drawstring sweat pants and loose-fitting shirts were the only things I wanted to wear.

One day a friend stopped me and said, "What's going on with you? Your skin looks great; it's like you have this special glow." That was right about the time I felt my baby move. Keith and I were so excited, and he never missed a chance to tell me I looked beautiful.

NORMAL CHANGES

I hope it helps to know that almost every pregnant woman goes through these physical symptoms and emotional changes. We get many letters at the Web site that say much the same thing. Here's an example:

> *Dear Becky,*
>
> *I'm seventeen years old and seven months' pregnant. Things are going OK, except that my life has really changed. I go to the doctor for a checkup once a month. I'm eating healthier food, which isn't easy for me, but I know I have to for the baby's sake. Sometimes I get very emotional—usually on the same days I feel fat and ugly. But my boyfriend says I look beautiful, and my mom tells me these feelings are normal.*
>
> *Your story and many others inspired me to make the right decision. I'm really excited about having my baby. I never thought I could do this, but now I'm convinced I'll be a good mom. So thank you.*
>
> *Dianne*

By the *sixth month* my friends knew I was pregnant, so I didn't have to feel so stressed about hiding it. As my belly got bigger, it began to itch—the doctor said it was from the skin stretching—and my lower back ached. I bought a pair of comfortable walking shoes and did some special exercises for my back. I also learned to sit down when I felt tired or sore.

At first it scared me when I felt some pain down the sides of my belly. Thank goodness I had a doctor's visit the next day. He assured me that I wasn't in early labor. He told me that as the baby grows, the uterus stretches the ligaments that support it. That explained the pain.

Fear like that may seem silly to some people, but when you don't know what's happening to your body, your imagination kicks in and thinks up all kinds of weird scenarios. That's why we're writing this chapter, so you'll know at least some of what is going on.

After that I sort of took things in stride. I kept all my doctor appointments, but they were usually over so fast that we didn't have time to discuss everything. So as my baby grew and each new symptom developed, I grabbed my pregnancy book, looked it up and usually followed the advice.

For constipation the book said to drink more water, eat more fiber—it's a good thing I like fruits and vegetables—and exercise more often. For heartburn I learned to eat small meals four or five times a day instead of pigging out in the cafeteria at lunch and dinner. The book also said not to take antacids without asking the doctor, but I found a glass of water cured my heartburn just as well as anything else.

In the *seventh month* I started to gain weight more quickly. My breasts and belly seemed to expand every week, and those stretch marks I had dreaded did appear.

I'm happy to tell that you most of them faded or went away completely a few months after my little girl was born.

One thing you really need to know is that gaining weight and swelling are not the same thing. You'll know the difference when you see it. If your ankles and feet swell from standing too long, sit down and put them up on something. When you lie down, put some pillows under your feet. The swelling should go away. If it lasts for twenty-four hours, or if your hands or face suddenly swell up, be sure and call your doctor.[1]

This is also the month you might start feeling some false labor, called Braxton Hicks contractions. The contractions are usually light. They feel somewhat like cramps you might get before your period, but they don't last very long. If you have more than five in one hour, you should call your doctor.

This is also when it gets uncomfortable to sleep. You can still roll on one side if you tuck pillows here and there. Meanwhile the little one inside you practices aerobics all night long! The baby gets rest during the day, when the activity of your body rocks her to sleep. Most babies continue the role of night owl for the first three months of life outside the womb. Just remember that this doesn't last forever, and you will learn to cope.

GETTING READY

By the end of the *seventh month* you should start birthing classes. Ask your doctor for a referral. Most hospitals, some clinics and some private groups offer instruction on different forms of delivery and prepare you for what you'll experience during labor. If you aren't able to take a class, be sure to ask lots of questions at your doctor visits. You also can find some good books at the library or look up information on the Internet.

By *month eight* the top of your uterus will probably be pushed up just under your rib cage. You might have trouble eating a full meal because your stomach is compressed. I like to snack, so eating small portions five times a day was fine with me. I felt tired and out of breath because the baby was crowding my lungs.

Your breasts might start to leak this month. The fluid is called colostrum, and if you've decided to breast-feed your baby, this is what he or she will eat for a few days until your milk comes in.

Speaking of which, this is a good time to decide how you will feed your baby: breast or bottle. That way you can know what to do and have the supplies on hand when the baby comes. Keep in mind that a well-fed baby is a sleepy baby!

You can get information from a pregnancy center about breast-feeding versus bottle-feeding. Most doctors will tell you that breast-feeding is healthier for both you and the baby. Mother's milk contains natural antibodies that your baby needs to stay healthy after birth.

Babies are not born knowing how to nurse; they have to be taught, and so do you. A lactation specialist can show you how to help your baby latch on so he or she will get enough to eat and thrive. Most hospitals and birthing clinics have a lactation specialist on staff. Or you can contact La Leche League, an international organization dedicated to providing education, information, support and encouragement to women who want to breast-feed their babies.[2]

If you decide to bottle-feed your baby, there are lots of options. You can pump your own breast milk and put it in a bottle. Or after the baby is born, your doctor can give you a shot to prevent your milk from coming in and you can rely on formula for your baby's food. Today's formulas can be just as nourishing as breast milk. If you hold your baby close in the nursing position while giving a bottle, the bonding experience between the two of you can be just as awesome.

SIGNS OF LABOR

You'll probably visit your doctor two more times during the eighth month. He'll most likely give you a heads-up on what to watch for in case of early labor, but I'll list them here just in case.

- bleeding or a gush of fluid from your vagina
- cramps, stomach pain or a dull backache
- blurry vision or spots before your eyes
- a feeling that the baby is pushing down
- a noticeable decrease in the baby's movements
- more than five contractions in an hour[3]

If you have any of these signs, call your doctor immediately. He will probably want to check you out, so if he asks you to go to the hospital, go! It's much better to have a false alarm than to ignore your symptoms and not be able to make it to the hospital on time.

Karla had two false alarms with her first baby. When

she finally went into true labor a week or so later, it was twelve hours before her daughter was born.

She was about thirty-eight weeks along with her second baby when her back started to ache and she felt the baby pushing down hard. She didn't want to go to the hospital and be sent home again. "That was so embarrassing," she told me later. "Besides, I'd had such a long labor with Sarah that I thought it was no big deal, even if this was the real thing." So she lay down to take a nap.

A few minutes later Karla felt as if she had to go to the bathroom. By the time she realized this *was* the real thing, it was too late.

"It was awful," she said. "I had to push—my body wouldn't let me stop—and the baby just fell out! Thank God my husband ran in and caught him before he hit the bathroom floor."

The paramedics arrived in time to deliver the placenta, then took mom and baby to the hospital in separate ambulances. Both of them were fine, but Karla was mortified. "If I ever get pregnant again," she said, "I swear I'm going to check into the hospital at eight months along and stay there!"

The story is funny now, and I don't tell it to scare you, just to make the point: It's worth a little embarrassment to be sure both you and your baby experience a safe delivery.

Who knows, the baby might surprise you by coming early. Most babies born at thirty-two to thirty-six weeks survive, though they may have to spend some time in an incubator.

THE REAL THING

Month nine, yes! I couldn't believe it was almost over. It seemed as if I had just found out that I was pregnant. Keith and I were married, and I was done with school for a while. This was a good thing, because by now the baby was so big that I felt uncomfortable. The skin over my abdomen was stretched so tight that my belly button stuck out.

I was seeing the doctor every week now, so I knew my baby had turned and dropped head-down into the birth position. I would have known that anyway because of the pressure of her head against my cervix. I constantly felt as if I had to urinate because she was pressing on my bladder too. I couldn't walk very far or very fast and had to rest often. Everything I read told me this was normal. I knew I just had to "hang in there" a few more days.

As much as I wanted to see and hold my baby, I was a little scared of the labor and delivery. I knew the symptoms and what to do, but no head knowledge can prepare you for the actual experience.

I went into false labor about a week before the due date. We thought for sure that this was it! Keith broke out the video camera and started to tape the entire experience: "Becky's in labor now. It looks like tonight's the night we are finally going to meet our little girl." He was so excited.

The next frame shows a tired and disappointed husband. "Well, Becky didn't have the baby, so I guess it was a false alarm." As if it was my fault! Poor Keith. If this is your first baby and the father is with you, remember that it's his first time too. He will probably be even more nervous, scared and excited than you are.

The "real thing" happened a week later. Yes, my daughter was born on her due date! When the contractions were about ten minutes apart and regular, we went to the hospital. Once they took me to the maternity ward, they asked me about my labor symptoms, then hooked me up to a machine that would monitor the duration and intensity of my contractions and also keep track of the baby's heartbeat.

As the contractions came closer together and became more intense, the nurses moved me to the delivery room. Keith held my hand, fed me ice chips and rubbed my back when I needed it. Best of all, he kept assuring me that everything would be OK.

If your baby's father can't be with you, then whomever you've chosen to be your labor coach will do the same things. It could be a relative, friend or the nurse on duty. It really helps to have someone by your side.

Labor is painful. My mom had done this a few times, so she knew that trying to fight the pain would only make things worse. She told me to relax and surrender to the pain. I needed to stay focused and peaceful.

Right! At one point I swung my legs over the edge of the bed and struggled to my feet. "Let me out of here!" I yelled at Keith. "This is too hard!" I grabbed my pants and started to put them on. "I've had enough; I want to go home." I knew I was being totally irrational.

Thank God Keith stayed calm. He spoke softly, and he patiently helped me back to bed. We can laugh about this now, but it sure wasn't funny then.

JOY TO THE WORLD!

Finally the doctor told me I could push, and I felt a new surge of energy. It wouldn't be long before this would be over and I could hold my baby. "OK, baby," I whispered, "we can do this." For a half hour I focused and pushed, then our beautiful baby girl was born. We did it! I laughed and cried at the same time!

What indescribable joy I felt at the moment the nurse placed her on my chest. I looked down into her little face and saw Keith's lips and hair, my nose and cheeks. She was a perfect combination of the two of us. How miraculous is that?

Now that I have gone through labor and delivery, the fear of the unknown is gone. Believe me, fear only makes pain worse, so remember what you've learned and stay calm. I prayed a lot, and so did Keith. And we knew our family and friends were praying too. That helped a lot.

The best part of all was when we took our baby, Joy, home. I'd never seen Keith drive so carefully! We had precious cargo on board, and it was his job to protect her.

When we walked through the door, reality hit with an overwhelming sense of awe. I remember thinking, "This little girl belongs to us!" Joy is ours to love, nurture, protect and teach until she is ready to be on her own.

Thank God that this is a gradual process. He has given us approximately eighteen years to be the most important influence in her life. We pray every day that we will do the job well.

KEY QUESTION:

What are some changes you need to make in order to have a healthy pregnancy?

CHAPTER ELEVEN

STAND UP GIRL!

I used to be judgmental of girls who got pregnant outside of marriage—until I did. I looked down on any girl who even considered abortion—until I had to make some hard choices. I've learned many things through my experience with an unexpected pregnancy, but one of the most important is to not judge others. No one can know how he or she will feel or act in a crisis situation until it happens. The only reason I can offer you advice on the Web or in this book is because I've been where you are.

Many of the letters we get from girls in crisis pregnancies speak of fear and anxiety about the changes that lie ahead. My life changed in many ways, but the thing that scared me the most was what people would think about me when they found out. I was afraid my parents would disown me and my friends wouldn't want anything to do with me anymore. I was so embarrassed that I hid my pregnancy from my classmates as long as I could.

When my friends finally did find out, they were there for me, but many times they just didn't know how to act around me or what to say. My lifestyle had changed, and theirs hadn't. We had so little in common now.

Our usual hangout had been the local pub, but I lost interest in going there. I couldn't have even one drink, and I knew the secondhand smoke was bad for the baby. Besides, I was usually too tired to stay out late. My friends quit asking me to go places. Many of them drifted away, and I admit that for a while I felt left out.

I decided to focus on school, and my grades really improved! My parents and professors were impressed, which made me feel good about myself. At the same time I learned the difference between real friends and acquaintances. My true friends didn't judge or condemn; they just loved me. They listened when I needed to talk. They prayed with me and stood by me through each decision I made. These are the friendships I will treasure for a lifetime.

As my baby grew and my body changed, I recognized that my purpose and direction in life had changed as well. My goals were different, focused more on others, especially the baby and my future husband. I focused on my role as a mother and a wife. Pushed beyond the comfort of a small-town college world, I gained self-confidence and realized that I didn't have to go with the crowd to feel good about myself.

How will your pregnancy change your life? You're the only one who can answer that. I can promise it won't be easy, but remember that old saying "Every cloud has a silver lining." If you choose to try, you'll find that something good can come out of even the worst situation.

IT'S UP TO YOU!
The following letter from Kathy is an example of good choices made under difficult circumstances.

> Dear Becky,
>   My boyfriend and I attended the same private college. We were both honor students involved in school government. When I got pregnant, the

*administrator advised us that we had to resign
our leadership positions. He also withdrew letters
of recommendation to companies that would have
launched our respective careers. When I protested,
he told me I should have had an abortion and not
said anything. We were basically blackballed in
the school community because we chose to keep
our baby. Our well-laid plans for travel, careers
and a carefree future crashed down around us like
bricks in an earthquake.*

*That's exactly how it felt: like we'd been in an
8.5 on the Richter scale and the ground would
never stop shaking. If our families hadn't been
there, I don't know what we would have done.
We were still dependent on them for housing
and finances, but we also needed them to stand
with us, help us with decisions and love us
through it all.*

*Everyone else was so cold! Most of our
classmates snubbed us, even though I knew that
many of those girls had taken their daddy's
money for "an afternoon of shopping" and
returned "feeling sick." Their parents never knew
the difference, and if the school officials knew,
they looked the other way. That was what they
preferred: If the girl dealt with "the problem" right
away, then the school would not have to get
involved.*

*We stuck it out. I cried through most of my
pregnancy but kept up with my grades so I could*

*graduate. My boyfriend studied and worked a
part-time job.*

*It took over two years, but our world finally
settled on a much stronger foundation. The jolt of
an unplanned pregnancy taught us a great deal
about family and relationships. We learned the
meaning of perseverance in the face of hardship.
We came to understand that independence
requires responsibility and real love is
unconditional. We plan to teach these things to
our son.*

Kathy

Kathy and her boyfriend had lofty goals, and they could
have bowed to the so-called "wisdom" of others and "done
away with the problem." But they shouldered their responsibilities. They will move up the career ladder more slowly
than they had planned, but in the meantime, as Kathy
says, "we are truly thankful for the gift of our little boy."

GOALS AND GETTING THERE

What is your situation? What could be your silver lining?
Whatever your decision about your baby, it would be a
good thing to take a look at the future and set some rea-
sonable goals.

Obviously, if you've decided to keep your baby, married or not, your immediate future will include diapers and
baby clothes, a car seat and crib, late night feedings and
doctor bills. (If you're a first-time mom, a class or book on
infant care is a must. We will give you some suggestions in
the back of this book.)

What kind of goals can you set with all of that added to your schedule? Take stock of your situation. If you are still in school, one goal might be to finish and get your degree. You will need someone to help with child care and possibly financial support.

If you have to work to earn a living for your new little family—and you are a family even if it's just you and baby—then you might have to postpone your education for a while. I dropped out of college to be a full-time mom. Keith found a job, and our parents helped us with housing. Our major goal was to find a way to be financially independent and give our child the best possible chance in life. It has taken a while, but we have, with God's help, achieved that goal.

Maybe your goal is just to survive until your baby is born. If so, take it day by day. Your obvious needs are food, shelter and prenatal care. If that's all you concentrate on, then that is a step in the right direction.

There is help for you out there. Take some time to think about and write down your options. Is there a social services agency in your community? Do you have a friend or relative who can be there for you?

FINDING SOMEONE TO CARE

For Sara and Carrie it came down to life on the streets or finding help quick.

We were only fourteen, but all our friends had already done it with a boy. We decided it would be fun to lose our virginity at the same time. There were these cute boys we all hung out with, so it was easy to do.

Then we decided it would be fun to take a
pregnancy test. We bought two apiece. When the
first ones were positive, we laughed. We thought it
was just a dud. But when the second tests were
positive, we freaked.

The boys just said, "Get out of here." They had
used condoms, and besides, you can't get
pregnant your first time. Wrong!

My parents threw my things into the street.
Sara's mom packed her clothes in a suitcase and
shoved her out the door. We spent the night under
a freeway overpass. In the morning I knew we had
to do something, so we called my grandma. I
think she was madder at my mom than me, but
we sure had to listen to a lecture. We stayed with
her until the babies were born.

Carrie knew they could not stay with her grandmother forever. Both girls knew they weren't ready to raise a baby.
Sara's mom and Carrie's grandmother helped them find
adoptive homes.

The girls still had to come up with a plan to finish
school. Thankfully, Sara's parents relented and allowed
her to come home. It wasn't easy because their relationship had been damaged, but Sara realized that was the
only way she could get on with her life, so she stuck it out.
Carrie went to live with her older sister and completed her
GED in two years.

No matter what the outcome of your pregnancy, there
will be pain and hardship, anger and tears. But as the Bible
says, "Weeping may linger for the night, but joy comes

with the morning" (Psalm 30:5). Your circumstances might seem insurmountable right now, but if you take time to think and plan, and especially pray, things will get better. There is a right road for each one of us. We just have to *stand up* and find it.

WHAT ABOUT SEX?

Speaking of the future, there's another decision to make. This one is huge and can have another life-changing impact on you and your baby's future. Yes, I'm talking about sex. Should you or shouldn't you?

My advice is to wait until you are married to have sex. When people used to tell me that, I remember thinking to myself, "You don't understand. I really love this guy!" We did love each other, but God loves us much more, and he created sex and the binding of marriage that sanctions it. So we abstained from sex until we were married.

Some girls say it's impossible to stay celibate once you've had sex, but I know that's not true. It's not easy, that's for sure, but the decision to stay sexually active is a choice, not a given.

Maybe your baby's father has been there for you all along. Maybe you choose to continue your sexual relationship without getting married. Maybe one of you will get tired of the relationship and leave. After all, there is no commitment or marriage document to hold you together. Divorce happens all the time, even to those who go into marriage with the best intentions.

Without the commitment of marriage, you could find yourself back in the same heartbreaking circumstances:

another pregnancy, another baby, another tough decision regarding your baby's life and your own future. You have another chance to do things right, so be smart.

A GRAVE DANGER

Another dragon raises its ugly head. What do you know about sexually transmitted diseases (STDs)? You may be clean now, but the more sexual partners you have, the more likely you are to catch one of these dreaded diseases. It's just as important to get an education about the risks of sexual diseases as it is to know the risks of abortion.

Right away we all think about AIDS. The media would have us believe that condoms protect people from the HIV virus. But this virus is much smaller than sperm, so it is more likely to escape through even a small hole or tear in a condom. Scientific data proves that condoms are only 87 percent effective in preventing pregnancy. How effective can they be in preventing AIDS?[1]

Just a few years ago there were only a few known STDs. Genital herpes, syphilis and gonorrhea were the most common. Now the list has grown to include HPV (human papilloma virus), chlamydia, trichomonas, hepatitis B and hepatitis C as well as others. Some of these STDs can lead to pelvic inflammatory disease, cervical cancer and even death.[2]

Another problem is that people with the most common STDs—chlamydia, genital herpes and human papilloma virus—are contagious before they have symptoms! In these cases the phrase "pass it on" has a whole new meaning.

I'm not really into statistics, but the facts make me cringe. A report from the Medical Institute for Sexual Health says that over sixty million Americans have at least one STD, and fifteen million new cases occur each year. Two-thirds of these new cases are found in people under the age of twenty-five. That's just in America.

For a person who has an active sex life with more than one partner, the odds of being infected with a sexually transmitted disease are high. Think about it: If you decide to sleep with Joe, and last week Joe slept with Sally, and the week before that Sally slept with Fred, your chances of catching an STD are multiplied several times. That's risky.

Like abortion, STDs can not only make you sick; they can make you sterile. And if you should get pregnant, the baby could suffer from that same disease. Marriage won't make the consequences go away. Only a commitment to one lifetime "clean" partner can keep you free from sexual disease.

If you rely on condoms to protect you, think again. It's true that if you use a condom 100 percent correctly, 100 percent of the time, your risk of contracting HIV is reduced by about 85 percent. But your chances of being infected with gonorrhea, chlamydia, herpes and syphilis are reduced by just 50 percent. Condoms do not protect you from HPV at all.[3]

I guess the bottom line is that we live in a scary world. So much can go wrong. I don't know about you, but for me sex with anyone but a lifetime partner is just not worth the risk.

STAY STRONG

Cheryl came to regret her sexually active lifestyle, and she has made some positive decisions. She just hopes it is not too late.

> *I am almost twenty-four and have a two-year-old son who has some serious disabilities. I left his father about six months ago, and one week later I met another guy. We had sex only once and used a condom, but I got pregnant anyway! When I said no to abortion, he walked away.*
>
> *Then I met a man who wanted to be together and accepted my pregnancy, but I am afraid to have a relationship with him. One day I want to get married and have a family, but I already have two children with two different dads. I have to wonder if I will ever find someone willing to marry me and take on so much responsibility.*
>
> *I have never been a strong believer in God, but now I have found myself turning to him for help. So far, tests for a sexually transmitted disease have been negative, but I don't want to up the risk. So until I find the right man to marry, I will have to stay strong, stay abstinent and take care of my children by myself.*

Deidra and her boyfriend were sexually active, but because they stayed faithful to each other, they escaped the consequence of STDs. They realize their age is against them, but both are determined to make their marriage work. She writes:

My boyfriend and I had been together for over three years, but we were both only seventeen and still in high school when I got pregnant. We took a stand and refused to abort our baby. We loved each other and we both had jobs; there was no reason we couldn't be a family.

Because we had been together so long and neither of us had ever had another sexual relationship, our parents gave their consent for us to get married. They helped us rent a little one-bedroom apartment. We have one more year of school and it is a hard road, but I know we will make it, because we are both determined that our baby and our marriage come first.

Tami met Dan after they had both graduated from college. Dan was Tami's first lover, and they planned to marry "someday." She knew he'd been around but did not realize how his previous sexual activity would affect her life.

I have decided that abortion is out of the question. I'm the one who has to face the consequences. I told my boyfriend it wasn't worth the risk. He can offer me money or say, "I'm sorry," a million times, but it won't change the situation. He's the one who gave me herpes. Our baby is at risk, but that's not reason enough to kill him or her.

We've been together a long time. He says he loves me. I say, take the abortion money and get a marriage license. He's been out of town for a week and has had plenty of time to think about it. We

aren't kids; we need to stand up to our
responsibilities and give our child a family. I hope
and pray we can agree. If not, I will have to leave
him and do this on my own. That's not what I
want either, but I am determined to do what is
right.

Now, that's what I call a Stand Up Girl!

CHOOSING PURITY

I know of other young women who learned the hard way to make some serious choices about sex.

Kaylee had her baby at fifteen. Her boyfriend walked away from the relationship, but both families have stepped in as devoted grandparents and made it possible for Kaylee to finish high school and move on to college. She is determined to stay celibate until she finds the man she is supposed to marry.

Celeste had a new boyfriend every year until she turned twenty. That's when she discovered she had HIV. It has not yet turned into full-blown AIDS, but she will never have a child, nor can she in all good conscience have sex with or marry anyone who doesn't already have the disease. She uses all her spare time to share the value of abstinence with middle school and high school students.

I made a mess out of my life, and there was no way even Keith could make it all better. For weeks I tortured myself with what ifs. What if we hadn't slipped? What if we had stayed apart when we realized our feelings were out of control? We should have stayed with a crowd of friends and not put ourselves into a tempting situation. I should have stayed at school and not gone home during breaks. And on and on and on.

Finally I realized I needed to stop beating myself up over the poor choices I had made. I felt overwhelmed with responsibility for this new little life I carried inside. There were days I stumbled and would have given up if it weren't for God. He brought people into my life to help when I needed it.

There's a song that says, "God sees each tear that falls. He hears you when you call." Believe me, there were tons of tears and lots of cries for help. He heard each one and gave me the strength I needed to live day by day and moment by moment.

PRAY FIRST

For me motherhood is a privilege, a special gift. I can't tell you enough how much I cherish each moment with my Joy. Being a mom isn't easy, but even tough times are worth it because I know she is worth it. God has a special plan for her life, and I am part of that plan. What could be more awesome than that?

Now a word to those of you who don't see anything awesome about any of this, let alone any type of positive plan.

Kim is one of you. She writes:

I am eighteen, a 4.0 student and popular in school. My dad is the pastor of the biggest church in town, and my family is in the spotlight, so to speak. We have a code of rules to follow because people look up to us and we can't cause any

*offense. How in the world am I supposed to tell
anyone I'm pregnant?*

*I have no money of my own, so I can't just
disappear. The baby's father is no longer in my
life. I'm desperate because it's getting harder to
keep this a secret. I vomit every day. I'm always
tired and so weak I can barely make it through
a day.*

*I don't feel any strong connection to the life
inside me, but I believe abortion is murder; still, I
don't see any other way. I desperately need help,
but it will have to be from a stranger. Please, can
you give me some advice?*

I was able to tell Kim that I understood her fear. My dad
held a prominent position in our church. I'd always been
the kind of girl who made my parents proud, one my siblings could look at as a role model. I truly believed that sex
before marriage was wrong and that abortion was murder,
but when I got pregnant, fear of what people would think
or do drove me to the same frantic desperation as Kim.

I advised Kim to pray for courage and go to her parents
with a repentant attitude. "When you talk with them about
your pregnancy, I promise you'll feel better. No matter
how they react, at least you'll have that burden off your
shoulders."

I also asked her to think carefully about her options.
"Please don't go against your own heartfelt beliefs. If you
do, I know you'll regret it for the rest of your life."

FROM DESPAIR TO HOPE

I think Maria's story proves this point:

> *In my culture a woman marries very young. To be eighteen and single is an embarrassment to the woman and her family. I wanted so badly to be a wife and mother. So I decided, "If I am pregnant, the baby's father will marry me." But when I am pregnant, the baby's father put me aside. My father beat me. I must obey and have an abortion.*
>
> *Three times I am pregnant, three times the baby's father turns away, my father beats me, and I have all together three abortions.*

When an older man offered to marry Maria and take her away from the abuse she endured at home, she accepted. "I felt such joy," she said. "I think, 'Finally my dreams have come true.' But then the doctors say I will never have a baby. I am scarred from the abortions and will not carry a child."

Her husband assured her they could adopt a baby, but the pain and guilt Maria carried in her heart caused her to go into a deep depression. Her grief nearly drove her to suicide. Finally, in her mid-thirties, Maria found a compassionate post-abortion counselor who helped her understand that God had forgiven her, then taught her how to forgive herself.

"I have made many mistakes," Maria said, "but God had a plan. My husband shares my dream to have many children. Now we return to our own country. There are many abandoned babies, and we make a home for them."

Maria and her husband have started an orphanage near the village where she was raised. Now she is not only a homemaker and helpmate to her husband but a mother to many children, all of whom she loves as if she had given them life.

FINDING GOD'S PLAN

Do you believe God has a plan, not just for you but for your baby as well? Read the following story and see what you think.

It starts in 1968, when a couple in their late forties discovered they were going to have another child. They felt they were too old to raise a baby. Abortion wasn't legal then, but it was possible to have it done. A friend offered to introduce them to a doctor who would "take care of the problem."

The couple couldn't bring themselves to get rid of the baby. After a complicated pregnancy the woman gave birth to a baby boy. The boy's father died when the child was fifteen, and the mother did the best she could to raise him. As soon as he turned eighteen, the boy was on his own.

A few years later, in a different part of the country, a young woman was suffering an extremely high-risk pregnancy. The doctors and specialists agreed that the baby wouldn't live and the mother was in danger. They urged her several times to let them take the baby. Determined to have her child, she stood her ground. After enduring five months of endless suffering, her baby boy was born. Brain damaged, partially blind and physically disabled, the doctors now predicted he would be a vegetable.

His mother disagreed. She read to him, sang to him and took him from one doctor to another seeking hope. The child grew. He learned to walk and speak. His hearing was fine, and he understood what was said to him. He loved motorcycles and cars, puppies and anyone who would give him hugs.

Everyone said she was killing herself taking care of this little boy who would never grow up. They all said he'd be better off in an institution so she could get on with her life. Instead she put him in a special education class, and he rides the school bus with other special needs kids.

Then she met the man whose older parents had chosen to give him life. This man fell in love with her and with her little boy. He stepped right in to give them the help they needed, and together they provide love, joy and hope for a precious child.

The point is, we don't know what or whom God will use to carry out his plan. Our job is simply to trust him and allow him to work it out.

UNEXPECTED BLESSINGS

I'll end this chapter with a letter from a woman who has been where you are. She took a stand for life, had her son and raised him with the help and support of family and friends. Now she reaches out to others.

Even though I did not expect to get pregnant, I could not consider abortion. I know I did wrong, but that is not my child's fault. God blessed me with a healthy little boy, and I would not trade a minute of his life for an easier road.

One day a fifteen-year-old girl came to my church. She was three months' pregnant, her mother had kicked her out, and she had nowhere to go. At the end of the service, she asked the pastor if the church could help her. He looked at me and smiled. I knew what I had to do.

With help from the church we gave her a home and helped her get a grip on life. Her baby is now a year old, and she still lives with me. She has a good job and is finishing her high school education. When the time is right, she will make it on her own. Meanwhile, we fill the role of family in her life. It's been a blessing for everyone involved.

When you stand up for what you know is right and make positive changes in your life, believe me, others will notice and follow your example. When you *stand up* and say no to premarital sex, you will be safe from the consequences of STDs or another unexpected pregnancy. Both you and your baby will benefit when you *stand up* and take responsibility for your life. And you can help other women *stand up* too.

KEY QUESTIONS:
What positive changes do I need to make?

In what ways can I take a stand for life?

How can I help someone else avoid the mistakes I have made?

PART FOUR

FOR THOSE YOU LOVE

CHAPTER TWELVE

FOR MOM AND DAD

Of all the unmarried pregnant women who have written to me, none have ever said, "I can't wait to tell my parents." As you have read in the previous chapters, fear of what Mom and Dad will say comes directly after the shock of a positive pregnancy test.

For women who are young, the reason is obvious: They depend on their parents for food, shelter and all of their daily needs. For women of any age, I believe there is a deep-seated need to respect and please the ones who gave us life. Let's face it, the truth is that it hurts to disappoint our parents.

Even when we feel rebellious, it isn't our intent to hurt them; we just want our own way. And our own way often gets us into trouble. We think our parents are "clueless," but they have lived longer and have more life experience than we do. And just maybe that's why they make the rules we so hate to follow.

When it comes to facing a crisis, most of us have always turned to our parents, even when we knew they might be angry. Maybe you broke the neighbor's window with a poorly aimed softball or backed into a tree with your father's new car. Sure, it was hard to confess those misdeeds, especially when you knew there would be consequences. But you knew they would find out, so you admitted your mistake and accepted your punishment as a matter of course.

So what makes it so much harder to go to our parents with the news of an unexpected pregnancy? I believe it is because all the other mistakes we made as children were "fixable." Mom and Dad took the money for the window out of our allowance or confiscated the car keys for a week, and then it was over. But this time the mistake is not "fixable." Our parents can't rewind the clock and undo our mistake.

Not only that, but our parents have the power to help or hurt us. When their idea of how to solve the problem is different from ours, the conflict causes a rift in our relationship with them that can be difficult to mend.

The point of this chapter is to offer your parents insight into your thoughts and feelings and offer some suggestions as to how they might help instead of hurt. I hope they will read this book with you. It may answer many of their questions as well as yours.

THANKS FOR EVERYTHING

The following letter is one I wrote to my own parents after our baby, Joy, was born. I hope it will give your mom and dad some insight as to how your life might change for the better when your baby is born.

> *Dear Mom and Dad,*
>
> *Having just experienced the beautiful miracle of pregnancy and the birth of my daughter, it's much clearer what you went through to bring me into the world, and I want to thank you for choosing life for me. Thank you also for raising*

me to know God. You taught me from a young age that nothing could separate me from his love. I know he forgives all of my failures. He has entrusted me with this precious child, and he is my source of strength.

I also want to thank you for all of the support you gave me during my pregnancy. It meant so much to know that you were behind me all the way. Even though I didn't live close to you, I knew that you would be willing to talk on the phone any time, day or night.

Thanks, Dad, for taking the time every Friday to call me. Those conversations were often the highlight of my week. I feel like I can talk to you and Mom about anything. I still have so many questions, and it's a comfort to know that you are there with words of wisdom and encouragement. Your sense of humor lifts my spirits on days when I struggle to put one foot in front of the other.

Thank you, Mom, for your love and your example. Your unselfish love for your family is such an inspiration to me. Thank you for all the sacrifices you've made for us. Thank you also for helping me to see that pregnancy and childbirth is not some big, scary thing, but rather it is something very natural and "doable." Your serenity gave me the courage I needed to go through the pregnancy and give birth. I drew such strength in knowing that you had done this eight times! Surely I could make it through this one.

I know it was hard for you to find out that I was pregnant. You wanted so much for me to do things in the proper order. I wanted that too, but I messed up. I'm sorry for the grief I caused you. I know that you were probably judged and looked down on by many people. It must have been really hard for you sometimes, but thank you so much for standing by me through everything.

I love you both so much and am glad to be your daughter.

Becky

HEARING THE NEWS

I realize how blessed I was to have parents who stood by me even though they were hurt and disappointed by my behavior. It must be a shock to hear the words "I'm pregnant" from the girl you thought was still a child, the one you had taught right from wrong, the one you thought would finish school, start a career, then maybe get married and have a baby—in that order. It's good to have expectations for your children, but things don't always turn out the way you think they should.

Most parents I've talked to express feelings of shock, anger, disappointment, resentment and confusion. "What am I supposed to do now?" is a phrase I often hear from moms and dads who have just learned about their daughter's pregnancy.

Your first reaction might be to express your feelings with hurtful words and actions. Your daughter knows that. Almost every girl I hear from expresses one of these statements: "I can't tell my parents because they will kill me." "I'm scared to tell my mom; she'll probably beat me and throw me out of the house." "I absolutely cannot tell my parents. They would be devastated." "My dad won't listen, and he'll probably kill my boyfriend." "My mom will never speak to me again."

The root of all of these statements is fear—fear of how you, Mom and Dad, will react. What your son or daughter does not realize, and you may not either, is that your immediate words and actions stem from the same emotion: fear.

An unexpected pregnancy is a major crisis that will change your life as well as your child's life forever. You might as well go out for dinner and come home to find your house burned down. All of your hopes and dreams for the child that you've raised have gone up in smoke. You gave her life, fed and clothed her, provided a home for her and paid for her education. You have a right to feel betrayed, angry, scared and even embarrassed.

You also have a choice.

All of her life you have met your child's needs. What your daughter needs most from you now is unconditional love and support. If you can't see it that way, or if you feel she should be held accountable for her actions and deal with this pregnancy on her own, please hang in there with me for a few minutes.

TIME OUT

Throughout this book we've advised your daughter to take time to sort through her feelings, examine her choices and plan for the options that will work best for her, her partner and the innocent life she carries. We advise her partner too to think hard about the future. May we ask you to do the same?

My parents reacted to Keith's and my confession with anger, harsh words and tears. Yet, once they got over the shock, they took time out to evaluate the situation. Now I'm asking you to remember that what you do and say will affect your child and your grandchild forever.

Your response will also affect your own future. One woman in her late twenties could not tell her parents about her second out-of-wedlock pregnancy because they had not spoken to her since she became pregnant with her first child. Her parents had split up right after that, and this young woman truly believed the divorce was her fault. These parents have a quadruple loss: They've lost each other, their daughter and two beautiful grandchildren. They have missed the thrill of a tiny warm body in their arms, the joy of an infant's first smile, hugs and kisses from a sleepy-eyed, pajama-clad toddler and the excitement of that first soccer game or dance recital.

Your child may be fourteen, eighteen or twenty-five. Age has no boundaries when it comes to unconditional love, mercy, forgiveness and acceptance, though it does affect the amount of help your child needs from you.

Please take time to read this book with your daughter and, if appropriate, help her make the best decision possible for everyone concerned. Remember, your support may mean the difference between life and death for your grandchild. Many girls have abortions just because they feel they are in this alone. Help your daughter understand that there are positive options. If she knows you are there for her, emotionally and physically, it will make it easier for her to choose life. How you respond now will influence the way your child handles his or her future relationships.

To parents of the father I say, please help your son know that you will be there for him. He too is responsible for the life of this baby. His immediate reaction also stems from fear, and though he may need your support in a slightly different way, he too needs guidance and love.

Christine is grandmother to a brand new baby girl. She didn't approve of her son's living with his girlfriend out of wedlock, and when she heard they were pregnant, she cried. These kids were in their twenties and on their own. Christine knew she couldn't change anything, so she decided to be supportive instead.

As she warmed to the thought of being a grandma, her feelings of love for her family took over. She visited often and helped out when her son's partner, now more like a daughter to her, had a difficult pregnancy. At one point they almost lost the baby, and Christine was there for them all the way.

"The value of life before birth is something I feel strongly about," she says. "Every time I look at my grand-baby, I am amazed that anyone could not count them as human. I was so very lucky to have seen her [in an ultra-sound] at sixteen weeks and see that everything was so perfectly formed! I love her so much and couldn't imagine life without her."

LEARNING FROM OTHERS
Parents, here are some testimonies from girls who found help from the adults in their lives.

I thought my mom would kick me out, but all she did was cry. She wanted me to get an abortion. When I refused, she begged me to consider adoption. I wanted to keep my baby, but she said I'd have to drop out of high school, and I might as well forget about college or any type of career. She said I'd have to live on welfare all my life, because there was no way she could support all three of us.

I'm the one who decided to leave. I moved in with my boyfriend, but he was so abusive, I finally moved back home. It was hard, but by then my mom had decided to help me as much as she could. Not only did I finish high school but college too.

I'm on my own now. I have a good job, my baby is healthy, and my mom loves her. When we visit on weekends, she can hardly put the baby down. I'm so glad she changed her mind. I know I couldn't have done it without her.

...

When I told my parents that I was going to have a baby, they just sat there in silence. I was nineteen, so even though the thought terrified me, I knew I might have to make a go of it alone. Then my father took a deep breath and said, "Well, it will be nice having a baby around the house again." At that moment I knew that my baby and I would be just fine.

...

My parents had warned me not to date this older man, but I didn't listen, and at sixteen I got pregnant with his baby. I expected the worst, but thank God, I was in for some surprises. My boyfriend stayed with me! We were both against abortion and wanted to keep our baby, so he went with me to tell my mom.

My parents were divorced, so we told my mom first. I thought she would be angry and throw my boyfriend out of the house. Oh, she stood her ground—I was too young to get married—but she did support my decision to have the baby and took care of me while I was pregnant.

My dad was very disappointed in me and angry at my boyfriend. It took him a while, but once he accepted the fact that he was about to be a grandfather, he went out of his way to build a new relationship with me.

My baby was born a few weeks ago. I have to finish high school before my boyfriend and I can get married, but he is there for me and is a good father. Best of all, even though my parents are still divorced, we are a family again. So thanks, Mom and Dad, for helping me through the hard times. Our baby girl is so worth it!

It's important to remember that your children are your children forever. You gave them birth, changed messy diapers, doctored skinned knees and intervened when they had problems at school. You helped with homework, gave

them chores to help them learn responsibility and provided an allowance as a reward. You stayed up all night
when they were sick, took forgotten lunches or gym
clothes to school, applauded their successes and consoled
them when they failed. All their lives you have been there
when your children needed you. And they have never
needed you as much as they do now.

Mom and Dad, your daughter or son expects you to be
upset. Express your feelings, but please don't forget to
explain why you feel that way. Please take time out to sort
through your emotions and gain a perspective on the situation. Then get together with your son or daughter in a
quiet place to talk it over.

EXAMINING THE OPTIONS

Communication involves both talking and active listening.
So when you have expressed your feelings and well-
thought-out opinions, please listen to theirs. It's important
that both of you understand what the other is saying.
Don't be afraid to repeat what was just said in your own
words, then ask, "Is this what you mean?"

My parents gave me options at first that did not
include the choice Keith and I had made to marry right
away. Yes, we needed their help, but we also needed them
to support our decisions. When they realized we had
really thought things through and prayed about our decision, they gave us their blessing and their help.

If your child is very young, he or she may still be
dependent on you for food, shelter and clothing. He or she
may need more help than you are able to give. Don't be

afraid to get counsel! A crisis pregnancy center will be able to work alongside you to help your son or daughter with decisions and referrals to county agencies.

A child's crisis pregnancy changes your life too! You need love and support from someone who understands, so please don't be too embarrassed to seek help. If you can, find a friend who has "been there" and knows what you are going through. Believe me, you don't have to look very far to find someone who has walked in your shoes. Others have gone through this and found blessing and joy on the other side. A crisis counselor or your clergyman also might give you the support you need.

The bottom line is, no matter how old they are, your kids still need to hear, "I love you, I forgive you, and I'm here for you."

KEY QUESTION FOR PARENTS-TO-BE:
How can I help my parents understand how I feel?

KEY QUESTION FOR GRANDPARENTS-TO-BE:
How can I best help my child through this crisis pregnancy?

CHAPTER THIRTEEN

FOR YOUR BABY'S FATHER

Though your worst fear is probably your parents' reaction to the news of your pregnancy, your partner's response can cause you immense joy or unbearable pain. If this child is the result of a relationship with someone you love, you have willingly given to him your own body. Your mind and body are programmed to take that seriously.

God intended for the two to become one, and Jesus said, what God has joined together, no one has the right to separate (see Matthew 19:6). Of course, he meant that in the context of marriage. By going against God's best, you have put yourself in a vulnerable situation.

You might say, "We never really had a relationship; we were fooling around." As you now know, fooling around has its consequences. "Fooling around" might give a man the impression that the consequences are not his problem. He may feel no remorse at all when he leaves you alone and runs off to another conquest. In the meantime you are programmed to take your union with him more seriously. The result is heartbreak and pain.

I know it's easier to tell your story to a stranger than to tell the person with whom you have been so intimate how you feel about him and the baby in your womb. It's even harder to share your hopes and dreams for the future when you don't know what his reaction will be. This chapter is for you to share with your baby's father.

A LOOK AT THE LAW

Once in a while I get a letter from someone who says, "I am sixteen, and my boyfriend is twenty." If you are a man in such a situation, I have to caution you that you may be breaking the law. With or without the consent from the younger partner, in many states sexual intercourse between someone under eighteen and someone over eighteen is considered statutory rape.

Some states have a law called rape-3, which says that if one of the partners is under eighteen and the other is three years or more older, the older partner—usually the man—has committed a crime and may be prosecuted. That means that if the young woman is fifteen and the young man is eighteen or older, he has committed rape-3 and, if prosecuted, will possibly go to jail![1]

I'm not trying to knock you down here. It is important for you to know where you stand with your partner from a legal point of view. If I didn't care, I wouldn't share.

Dear Dad,

There are other things you need to understand about your relationship and responsibilities. So we've compiled the letters below to help you understand how your girlfriend might be feeling. My hope is that we will be able to help you understand your role in the decision-making process and come to terms with your relationship to your partner and your child.

...

Dear John,

Remember how scared we were when we found

out I am pregnant? We cried in each other's arms, and you promised me it would be OK. I trusted you because we were supposed to get married in a few months anyway, and I thought we would just move the date ahead a little. We both knew it would be rough financially, but I accepted your promise as a pledge that we'd somehow make it as a family— you, me and the baby.

When the doctor confirmed the results of the test, I cried because I was so happy and excited. I'd soon be your wife and a mother all at once! Do you have any idea how I felt when you asked the doctor how soon I could have an abortion? I was so shocked, I couldn't say anything even when you went ahead and made the appointment with an abortionist at the clinic. Then when we got to the car and you asked me what was wrong, I saw the look on your face when I said I wanted to keep our baby and raise it together. You hadn't meant it as a promise at all. You said, "We have to kill it! We can't start our marriage with a baby."

I lost it then. That's no news to you, but I want you to know that I meant what I said. I can never marry a man who would kill his own child. I will have our baby, but you will never be part of our lives.

...

Dear Joe,

I know you are right: we are not ready to have a child. I agree it was a mistake, but what are we going to do? It doesn't help when you won't take my phone calls. It's still your baby. How can you expect me to do this alone?

…

Dear Cal,

I'm still scared, but at least now both of our parents know. Thanks for coming with me. It made it so much easier to tell them together. Yes, my mom is still mad, and I don't think you'd better come over for a while. I don't want to give up our baby for adoption either, but I promised Mom I would at least look into it. We both know we're too young to get married, let alone raise a child.

BECKY WRITES TOO

Dear John, Joe and Cal,

You are different ages and at different stages in your lives, but I know you are all terrified at the prospect of becoming a father. Your plans for the immediate future did not include a baby.

Sex with your girlfriend was fun. Maybe you think that's just the way it is: guys need sex, and if a girl gets caught, that's her problem. Or maybe you really were in love until you discovered the consequences. You may think she's out to ruin your life, or you might really want to do the right thing, but you have no idea what the right thing might be.

The truth is that sexual intercourse, no matter what your age or how serious your relationship with the girl, can and often does result in pregnancy. Once is enough. Condoms break or come off. Your sperm joins with her egg and produces human life. A baby is a baby. New life is new life.

You can run from it, but that won't make it go away. It takes two to make it happen, and you, my friend, are the second half of the equation.

You might think abortion is the easy way out. I'm here to tell you that abortion is anything but easy. Abortion kills the baby you helped make and leaves emotional scars that both you and the baby's mother will have to live with the rest of your lives.

"But," you say, "I can't support a baby!" Or, "We're just friends; we were just fooling around." Whatever the scenario, it all boils down to this: You are the father of a baby. That means you have a responsibility to the mother and the child.

FINDING HELP

Steve understood that, but even though he felt committed to his girlfriend and their child, he didn't know what to do. So he did the smart thing: He sought help.

Dear Becky,

Please help! My girlfriend is pregnant, and I'm terrified. We aren't little kids, and I truly love her, but no way are we ready for a baby. We attend the same university and plan to marry after she graduates in two years, but for now we are pretty much dependent on our parents. She lives at home and doesn't have to work as long as she keeps up her grades. I survive on student loans, which I plan to have at least partially paid off by the time we marry.

My friends and family all tell us to get an abortion. I know Kate will never do that, and I don't want to either. I don't want to lose her. We've agreed to research the possibility of adoption. Maybe some other parents can give our baby a better home than we can afford right now. Kate's parents at least seem open to that idea. I love Kate and do want what's best for her and for this baby, but unless her parents relent and help us, I don't see any way out of this!

Steve

I hope my answer to Steve will help you sort out your concerns.

Dear Steve,

You won't regret the decision to give your baby life. I really admire you for your courage and your integrity. Your choice to support Kate 100 percent will make a huge difference in her life. Believe me, I know!

Now try and take things one step at a time. I think adoption might be a good thing to consider. There are so many couples who are searching for a

*child to adopt. You really have to think about
what is right for you and Kate though. My
husband and I started out with nothing. Neither of
us had jobs, and we were broke. Then people we
didn't even know came through with things for
our baby. I guess they could see that we were
trying hard to do the right thing.*

*I know you and Kate will discover the best
option for you. You will be in my prayers.*

Love, Becky

Steve, John, Joe and Cal, this book is also a resource for expectant fathers. Your girlfriend is reading it for information and education about all of your options. May I challenge you to read it with her? That way you too will find that there is help out there and an answer to your situation.

You and your baby's mother may not be able to maintain a relationship, but you can still *stand up*, be a man and take responsibility for the life you've helped create.

Maybe you want a relationship, but the baby's mother has other ideas. Maybe she has made a choice that you do not agree with. You may feel powerless, guilty or even depressed. Yes, men have these feelings too, and the key to resolving them is to admit they exist. Be honest with your partner about your feelings. Try to stay calm. When you are angry is not the time to talk. If she is adamant and refuses to listen, go to someone you can trust, preferably another man, and talk things out.

A friend might have some great advice, or his opinion might pull you in the wrong direction. He may sincerely want what is best for you, but a confidant with more life experience might be a better choice.

Our local crisis pregnancy center offers a mentor program for young fathers who are frustrated and don't know how to deal with their situation. There's a good chance you will find a program like that near you. (For the Care Net crisis pregnancy center nearest you, call 800-395-HELP.) Your pastor, priest or an elder at your church is another good option. Your school counselor or an understanding teacher can also be supportive.

No matter what the circumstances, if your girlfriend chooses abortion, you will also grieve. Dr. Vincent Rue writes, "For men and women alike, the feeling of emptiness [after an abortion] may last a lifetime, for parents are parents forever, even of a dead child."[2]

Forgiveness, of your partner and of yourself, will ultimately result in peace. There are people who understand and will help you. I hope you will seek them out.

DECIDE TOGETHER

May I say a word to the baby's mom? We've talked a lot about the hurt and fear you are going through. Because of hormones, the first three months of your pregnancy can be an emotional hurricane. It's all you can do to keep your own feet on the ground. But I would ask you to please remember that, even though he may not show it, your partner is also caught in a whirlwind of emotions. Carol reminds us that the two of you are in this together, no matter what the outcome:

*When I became pregnant with my fiancé's child,
he begged me to have an abortion. I felt trapped. I
cried every day and talked about suicide a couple
of times. My boyfriend said he couldn't take it
anymore, called off our wedding and moved out.
But when I made an appointment for an
ultrasound, he agreed to come.*

*The ultrasound showed our twelve-week-old
baby. We didn't know the sex until later, but as
we watched that day, she sucked her thumb. Then
when I poked my tummy a couple of times, she
actually stretched! We looked at each other and
cried.*

*When he took me home, we yelled and
screamed at each other. Then he sat down, put his
head in his hands and cried. When he could talk,
he told me he was scared, for us and for the baby.
He confessed he loved me but was afraid that no
matter what we decided, our relationship might
not survive because of the baby.*

*He agreed to go with me for counseling at a
crisis pregnancy center. We found out he was right
about one thing. The counselor told us that 70
percent of relationships fail within one month
after an abortion.[3] When we talked it out, we
realized that although it would be hard, we had
enough support to get married and keep our baby.*

If Carol's fiancé had not broken down and confessed his
feelings, she would have made her decision without him.
They may have lost each other and their baby. So please

recognize that your boyfriend shares the turmoil of your situation. Talk it out together, maybe with an older couple you can trust or with a professional counselor. Remember, the decisions you make together will affect your baby for the rest of his or her life.

Stand up, Dad. Be realistic, but be strong.

KEY QUESTIONS FOR MOM:

How can I help my baby's father understand our baby's needs?

How will his involvement in our lives help or hurt our baby?

KEY QUESTIONS FOR DAD:

How can I best help my baby's mother through her pregnancy?

What role will I play in my baby's life?

CHAPTER FOURTEEN

FOR FRIENDS

I'm sure you've heard the old saying "To have a friend you must be a friend." A friend laughs with you, even when the joke is not that funny, keeps your most cherished secrets, knows all of your faults and loves you anyway. A friend celebrates with you when you find that perfect job and helps pick you up when your best efforts are rejected.

When I was fifteen, my best friend and I met in front of our lockers after school. I don't remember what we were talking about, but out of the blue she announced, "Guess what? I'm pregnant."

"Yeah, right!" I snickered. She couldn't be pregnant. She wasn't even having sex. We told each other everything, and I would have known about that!

"No, really." She kind of half smiled. "I am. I even went to the doctor, and he told me I am."

I had no clue what to say.

The next day we acted as if nothing had happened. I tried to avoid her because I suddenly felt so awkward around her. A few weeks later she dropped out of school. I didn't see her much after that. Her world had changed, and I couldn't figure out where I fit in, so I just stayed away.

I did visit her after the baby was born and was awed by how mature she had become. She was a mother while I was still a girl in school. I admired her strength and courage, but could we still be friends?

I visited her again, and we talked about everything going on in our lives. After that we met often just to chat. I watched her little boy grow and saw her devotion to him. Too late I realized that I could have been there for her all along. I could have been a support to her and helped her through the rough parts. But my shyness and confusion kept me away.

A few years later I was pregnant and really needed a friend. I felt completely overwhelmed. In order to process things in my mind, I needed to talk them out. I needed someone to listen.

Remember those heart-to-heart talks at sleepovers? You will make a huge difference in your friend's life when you listen to her struggles, pain and regrets. I can tell you, she feels so alone! You can help her realize she isn't alone. Let her know you'll be there when she needs to talk.

You can help your friend understand that this isn't the end of the world. She can and will adapt to the changes in her body and in her life. You can help her keep her hopes and dreams alive.

"I'm here for you; how can I help?" Those words are a lifeline to a drowning friend. She may need someone with her when she tells her parents. She may need transportation to a doctor appointment or a partner for childbirth classes. She may even need a labor coach. She cannot do it all alone, and if you are there, she won't have to.

I needed prayer. My friends and I share the same faith. I know they lifted me to God every day. If prayer can move mountains, and I believe it does, then prayer can give your friend the hope and courage she needs to have this baby.

FRIENDS FOR LIFE

Lydia was blessed with some quality friendships. These young women knew how to help her and still hold her accountable. That takes maturity!

> *I have five good friends. I knew I could rely on them when I was down or just needed to talk. They didn't care about what others thought of me; they just cared about me. They didn't criticize me, but they did demand the best from me, which meant I had to make good choices during my pregnancy and stick to the decisions I made in the beginning.*

Melody's friend may have been a little naïve, but her heart was certainly in the right place.

> *My best friend cried when I decided to have my baby. When I asked her what was wrong, she said she was happy because she had made up her mind to find a way to adopt the baby so I wouldn't have an abortion. Can you believe that? She is no more ready to be a mom than I am!*

Now, that is a sacrifice of love!

No matter how old you are, a friend can be the most influential person in your life. Darlene writes:

> *I'm twenty-eight years old and the mother of a ten-year-old. Once again I am pregnant out of wedlock. I seriously considered abortion until I talked to a friend who had an abortion a few years ago. She said, "I know what abortion is all*

> *about. I also know you, and if you go through*
> *with this, it will kill you."*
>
> *I did some research, found your Web site and*
> *realized she was right. I am so thankful that my*
> *friend spoke up and said what I needed to hear.*
> *I'm excited about this baby and have been*
> *delighted with all the support I now have.*

If you've been there, *stand up* and share!

This young woman gives a great example of friends working together:

> *At first most of my friends thought I should have*
> *an abortion. Then one of them logged on to your*
> *Web site. We read the letters together, then took*
> *your advice. We found information about*
> *abortion at a pregnancy clinic, and I decided not*
> *to do it. Now my friends are really being*
> *supportive. They have even offered to baby-sit so I*
> *can finish school.*

FRIENDS TO FORGIVE

Talk about an unexpected pregnancy! Gail was forty-one, and her tubes had been tied when she delivered her twins thirteen years before. The doctor's exam confirmed that one fallopian tube had grown back together, and Gail was indeed pregnant with her fourth child. All the others were in their teens!

Gail and her husband did not really know what to do. Even with two incomes they could barely make ends meet. Abortion was totally out of the question, but how would they cope with another child to feed and clothe? Her teenagers pitched in to help with the chores, and her husband took a second job.

Gail's family and friends were as shocked as she was. Her best friend, Donna, decided to throw her a baby shower. Donna invited fifty of Gail's relatives, friends and coworkers and bought snacks, cake and door prizes. When the big day arrived, Donna cleaned her house and set out her grandmother's best china.

Only one person outside the family showed up, though no one had bothered to call and cancel. Gail's feelings were understandably hurt, and Donna was angry. She had hoped that Gail would receive all of the supplies she would need for a newborn. Two infant sleepers and a bag of diapers would nowhere near cover that need!

Gail and Donna could have indulged in a real friend-bashing session, but instead they chose to have an "attitude of gratitude." They opened the chips, dished up the cake, doled out the door prizes and basically had a great time.

At least Gail has Donna. Once in a while I hear from a girl who has absolutely no one on her side. So writes Missy:

When I found out I was pregnant, everyone turned against me. My mom sent me to live with a friend in a different state. I had to drop out of school and leave all my friends behind. I wasn't even allowed to have contact with any of them.

Mom's friend told me I was basically on my own. She gave me a room and showed me the

refrigerator. There was no way I could live like that
for eight more months, so I had an abortion.

I thought I could go back home and everything
would be OK. I didn't realize how depressed I
would get. I hate myself, my mother, her friend
and even my own friends, even though they really
didn't do anything wrong. Couldn't one of them
even have stood up for me?

Maybe you can step in for someone whose friends have deserted her. When Jennifer, a 4.0 student, discovered she was pregnant, she was forced to quit school. Her friends, including her boyfriend, dropped out of her life, and her parents told her she was on her own. She had her baby and worked two jobs to make ends meet.

Then a teacher from her old high school called her out of the blue and, no strings attached, offered her a scholarship to a four-year college and a loan to help make it until she graduated. Jennifer paid off the loan and now teaches third grade at her son's school.

Kyle and Dana also benefited from an adult friendship. They were two Christian kids who slipped up one time and were terrified when they discovered she was pregnant. Their youth pastor overheard them talking and offered to help. He arranged a meeting with the kids and their parents, then acted as mediator to help them sort it all out. He even helped them find a loving family to adopt the baby.

BE A FRIEND

Everyone needs a friend. Faced with the crisis of a surprise pregnancy, that need grows urgent. Friendship may be inconvenient and time-consuming, but it could mean the difference between life and death for a baby and a mom.

So your friend is pregnant. You've listened and helped her talk through her confusion and doubts. You've given her a shoulder to cry on and promised to "be there" for her whenever she needs you. But don't forget that she will still need friends after the baby is born.

There are dozens of ways you can help after the baby comes home. Like Donna, you could give your friend a baby shower. Even if she has baby clothes and blankets, there are bound to be other baby supplies she needs. Ask her for a list.

You can keep it simple and go in on one nice gift together with others or throw a larger event if she enjoys getting together with friends. You can e-mail, telephone, invite people in person or send out written invitations.

A follow-up phone call a day or two before the event is a must. People with the best of intentions can forget, so remind them about the party, where it's being held and what time it starts. If you leave things to chance, you may wind up like Gail and Donna with four teenage family members, one other friend, food and drink for fifty people and two presents.

If your friend is on her own, a simple offer to baby-sit will be a big help. Hold the baby while she takes a bath or a nap. Stay with the little one so she can shop or keep an appointment.

Do your homework together. Believe me, she can use another set of hands and eyes, not to mention someone with a clear mind. Her own is probably foggy from lack of sleep.

The list of practical helps is endless. Offer to do the dishes, run errands, bring her a meal or shop for groceries. Maybe she will welcome a ride to the doctor's office. If her family isn't involved, volunteer to be the one she calls in case of an emergency.

Whether she's married, living with family or on her own, the new mom will need encouragement. She needs someone to talk to and cry with. Being a mom is tough sometimes. A simple "You'll get through this" may be exactly what she needs to hear.

Your love, loyalty and support will help your friend *stand up* and take charge of her unexpected pregnancy.

KEY QUESTIONS FOR MOM:
Who are my closest friends?
How do I tell them what I need?

KEY QUESTIONS FOR FRIENDS:
What is my pregnant friend's most urgent need?
How can I help her?

FREQUENTLY ASKED QUESTIONS

The following questions are ones that we at StandUpGirl.com most often hear. They are listed alphabetically by category.

ABORTION

Q: Why do women have abortions?

A: There are many circumstances involved in a woman's decision to have an abortion, but the bottom line for most is *fear*. These women fear the unknown, the reaction of others, the loss of control over their own lives. They fear the changes that will certainly come—changes to their body and their life.

Often abortion is a matter of convenience. It is legal and easily obtainable. In much of society abortion is morally acceptable, while being pregnant out of wedlock is not. Many would rather kill their unborn baby than accept the responsibility that comes with "sexual freedom."

Lack of education is another reason for choosing abortion. Many women who face an unexpected pregnancy have not been given true or complete information on its risks and procedures. When they take the initiative to educate themselves about pregnancy and fetal development, many change their minds and decide to carry the baby to term.

A woman may panic when the child she carries is diagnosed with a birth defect or serious health problem. It takes a great deal of courage to choose life for a baby under those circumstances, but often the tests prove wrong. Even when the birth defect is not fixable, we are still talking about a human life with value.

Less than one percent of all abortions are performed because the child is conceived through rape or incest. Keep in mind that a baby so conceived is still a human being and innocent of any crime, but pressure from society to abort these babies is strong.

Q: What are the effects of abortion?
A: The physical risk for the baby is *death*.

The physical risks for the mother are many:
Hemorrhage: Heavy bleeding might require a transfusion, a second curettage procedure or a hysterectomy.

Infection: A uterus is susceptible to infection right after an abortion. The risk is even higher if the woman has chlamydia or gonorrhea. The symptoms of infection are pain and fever. If not treated with antibiotics, the infection could result in infertility or even death.

Perforation: If an abortion tool pushes through the wall of the uterus and damages one of the internal organs, major surgery may be necessary.

Complications of a continued pregnancy: If the baby is growing in a fallopian tube rather than in the uterus, the abortion would not be complete and the mother could be in grave danger.

Complications in later pregnancies: Severe injury to the cervix may result in the miscarriage of another baby, and uterine scarring could stop a fertilized egg from being implanted in the uterus. The risk of miscarriage in later pregnancies is higher if a woman has had two or more abortions.

Death: Heavy bleeding due to a perforated uterus and complications with anesthesia or chemical abortion drugs are the usual causes of death for the mother. Maternal death from a first-trimester abortion is rare. The risk increases in later-term abortions.

There are also emotional risks for the mother:
Sadness or depression: This can affect the woman's ability to cope with life.

Long-term grief: The cycle of grief repeats itself over a number of years.

Anger: This can include bitterness and hatred of herself and others.

Sexual dysfunction: This can lead to promiscuity or an aversion to sex.

Guilt: A woman may find it difficult to forgive herself or accept forgiveness from others.

Flashbacks: The woman relives the abortion and the events surrounding it.

Memory repression: The woman buries her emotions and convinces herself that the abortion did not happen.

Anniversary reactions: Grief and other emotional symptoms surface on the anniversary of the abortion or of the aborted baby's projected due date.

Hallucinations: A woman sees and hears what is not really there; a crying baby might trigger a need to find and nurture the lost child.

Suicidal tendencies: Some women are so scarred by the emotional reactions listed above that they are tempted to take their own life.

Increased alcohol and drug use: These may be used for the numbing effect and the illusion that being drunk or high will relieve emotional pain.

Difficulty keeping close relationships: Fear of loss pushes others away. Post-abortion stress syndrome can affect both men and women, but women are more likely to suffer severe symptoms. In most cases medical and psychological intervention is needed to restore emotional health.[1]

ADOPTION

Q: What is open adoption?

A: Open adoption allows for a relationship between the birthparents and the adoptive parents. The birthparents choose their child's adoptive parents from a list of families. The two sets of parents get to know each other through an agency or private lawyer, then reach an agreement as to how much involvement the birthparents may have in their baby's life. It can be anywhere from no involvement at all to letters, pictures, visits and so forth. [2]

Q: How do most adopted children feel toward their birth parents?

A: If the adoptive parents are open and honest with the child, answer his questions and assure him he is loved, most children respond with a positive outlook and take their adoption in stride. An older child who has not had ongoing contact with the birth parents may want to meet them. This can be stressful for everyone involved, but if the birthparents are open to a reunion, this usually results in closure for everyone and fills a void in the child's life.

LABOR AND DELIVERY

Q: Are labor and delivery always painful?

A: Labor is what the name implies: hard work. The muscles surrounding the uterus contract sharply to push the baby through the birth canal, while the baby stretches the cervix and vagina to their full extent. This can be a painful process, more so for some women than for others.

Breathing exercises, backrubs, whirlpool baths and medication can ease the discomfort. Sometimes a local anesthetic is given when the baby crowns or is ready to be pushed out. Your doctor or midwife will go over the process with you and help you select the best type of birth for you.

Q: What is "natural childbirth"?

A: The term simply refers to the experience of labor and delivery without medication or anesthesia. The mother is trained in methods of relaxation to help with the pain.

Q: Will pain medications during labor harm my baby?

A: Local anesthetics will not harm your baby. If you can get through labor and delivery without drugs, that is best, but unbearable pain may cause enough stress to tighten your muscles and delay delivery. That is not good for you and can harm the baby. So be wise, work out a plan with your doctor ahead of time and cover all the bases. Then be prepared to speak up or to take the doctor's advice if the plan must be changed.

LEGAL ISSUES

Q: Does my baby's father have the right to force me to have an abortion?

A: The woman alone has the legal right to decide for or against abortion.

Q: Can my baby's father stop me from releasing the baby for adoption?

A: The father has the right to contest an adoption in a court of law.[3]

Q: Do I have to put the father's name on the birth certificate?

A: The mother has the option to put "unknown" in place of the father's name. But the father can claim paternal rights in court and have the birth certificate changed.[4]

Q: Is the baby's father required to pay child support?

A: To establish child support and visitation rights, contact your local district attorney or legal aid office.

PARENTING

Q: How do I know I'll be a good parent?

A: A good parent provides his or her child with food, clothing, shelter, warmth and especially *love*. A good parent leads by example. A good parent educates herself about a child's physical and emotional needs and teaches the child how to function as part of society.

Parenting requires a lot of love, wisdom and patience. We can all grow in these virtues by practicing them.

Parenting is a "one step at a time" process, and thankfully there are many resources out there to help you. Look in Appendix B for some books we recommend. Talk to your own parents and parents of young children for advice.

Remember too that God has made you a parent of this child. He will give you the grace you need if you ask.

PREGNANCY

Q: How soon can I tell if I am pregnant?

A: To be certain of accurate results with an over-the-counter pregnancy test, you should wait until you've missed a period. Most pregnancy centers will test you as early as three weeks after the first day of your last period. A blood test done at a doctor's office or clinic can detect pregnancy as early as seven days after conception.

Keep in mind that there is a possibility of a false positive on any test, so be sure to have a doctor confirm a suspected pregnancy.

Q: What are the signs of pregnancy?

A: The earliest signs of a possible pregnancy are a missed period, sore and swollen breasts, nausea and fatigue.

ADDITIONAL RESOURCES

Abortion Information and Post-Abortion Help

For the Care Net crisis pregnancy center nearest you, call 800-395-HELP.

Crisis Pregnancy Help Line: 800-672-2296

Safe Place, a Post-Abortion Support Group: For confidential information call Pam, 541-998-7920.

Cochrane, Linda. *Forgiven and Set Free: A Post-Abortion Bible Study for Women*. Grand Rapids, Mich.: Baker, 1996.

Eggebroten, Anne. *Abortion, My Choice, God's Grace: Christian Women Tell Their Stories*. Carol Stream, Ill.: Hope, 1994.

www.standupgirl.com

www.optionline.org

www.pregnancycenters.org

www.abort73.com

www.care-net.org

Adoption

Horner, Susan and Kelly Fordyce Martindale. *Loved by Choice: True Stories That Celebrate Adoption*. Grand Rapids, Mich.: Revell, 2002.

www.courageouschoice.com

www.adoption.com

www.bethany.org

Girl Stuff

Murkoff, Heidi. *A Girl's Guide to Life: The Real Dish on Growing Up, Being True, and Making Your Teen Years Fabulous!* Nashville: Nelson, 2004.

www.lovematters.com

Parenting

"Children Do Come with Instructions." United Way of Lane County, 3171 Gateway, Springfield, OR 97477, Info@cherisheverychild.org.

Dobson, James. *Parenting Isn't for Cowards: The 'You Can Do It' Guide for Hassled Parents from America's Best-Loved Family Advocate.* Dallas: Word, 1987.

Murkoff, Heidi, Sandee Hathaway and Arlene Eisnberg. *What to Expect the First Year,* second edition. New York: Workman, 2003.

Reisser, Paul C. *No Fear Guide for First Time Parents.* Carol Stream, Ill.: Tyndale, 2002.

——. *The Focus on the Family Complete Book of Baby and Child Care.* Colorado Springs: Focus on the Family, 1999.

Pregnancy

Carr, Julie B. *Countdown to a Miracle: The Making of Me.* Marylhurst, Ore.: Motherly Way Enterprises, 2003.

Care Net Pregnancy Centers: 800-395-HELP.

Curtis, Glade B. and Judith Schuler. *Your Pregnancy Week by Week,* fifth edition. Cambridge, Mass.: Da Capo, 2004.

Dormon, Sara R. *I'm Pregnant...Now What?* Ventura, Calif.: Regal, 2002.

Flanagan, Geraldine Lux. *Beginning Life.* New York: DK, 1996.

The Good Housekeeping Illustrated Guide to Pregnancy and Baby Care, revised edition. New York: Hearst, 2004.

Iovine, Vicki. *The Girlfriend's Guide to Pregnancy.* New York: Pocket, 1995.

Murkoff, Heidi. *What to Expect When You're Expecting,* third edition. New York: Workman, 2002.

Nilsson, Lennart. *A Child is Born.* New York: Delacorte, 2003.

Shands, Linda. *What Now? Help for Pregnant Teens.* Wheaton, Ill.: InterVarsity Press, 1997.

Tsiaras, Alexander. *From Conception to Birth: A Life Unfolds.* New York: Doubleday, 2002.

www.teenpregnancy.com

Sex Education and STDs

www.lib.uiowa.edu/hardin/md/std.html

www.niaid.nih.gov/factsheets/stdinfo.htm

NOTES

PART TWO: YOUR OPTIONS

Chapter Seven: Abortion

1. This material on abortion procedures is taken from *Care Net Training Manual* (Eugene, Ore.: Lane Pregnancy Support Center, 2001), pp. 136–139. Care Net is a nonprofit organization that supports over eight hundred pregnancy resource centers in the United States and Canada. Care Net, 109 Carpenter Drive, Sterling, Virginia 20164. Phone: 703-478-5661. For the Care Net crisis pregnancy center nearest you, call 800-395-HELP. http://www.care-net.org.

2. John Ankerberg and John Weldon, *The Facts on Abortion: Answers from Science and the Bible about when Life Begins* (Eugene, Ore.: Harvest, 1995), p. 18.

3. *Care Net Training Manual,* p. 137.

4. Brochure "Making an Informed Decision about Your Pregnancy" (Grand Rapids, Mich.: Frontlines, 1994), 616-456-6874.

5. *Care Net Training Manual,* p. 137.

6. Nancy Gibbs, "The Abortion Pill," *Time,* October 9, 2000, p. 41–49.

7. *Care Net Training Manual,* p. 139.

8. "Making an Informed Decision about Your Pregnancy."

9. *Care Net Training Manual,* p. 139.

10. Gibbs, p. 44.

11. "Morning After Pill Label to Get Warning" (Washington: Associated Press, December 2004).

12. See Elizabeth Ring-Cassidy and Ian Gentles, *Women's Health after Abortion: The Medical and Psychological Evidence,* second edition (Toronto: deVeber Institute for Bioethics and Social Research, 2003), pp. 196–197.

Chapter Eight: Loss and Grief

1. Information about the stages of grief is taken from the American Association of Christian Counselors curriculum "Caring for People God's Way" (Forest, Va.: Center for Biblical Counseling).

Part Three: Facing Pregnancy

Chapter Nine: Your Baby

1. This information on fetal development is taken from Focus on the Family's brochure "The First Nine Months" (Colorado Springs, 1999).

2. Bethany Vaughn, "Pregnancy Milestones," www.icgold.net/mother/milestones.html.

3. "The First Nine Months."

4. Vaughn.

5. "The First Nine Months."

6. Stuart Shepard, "In-Utero Surgery Focus of Senate Hearing," www.family.org/cforum/fnif/news/a0028089. cfm, September 26, 2003.

7. Vaughn.

Chapter Ten: Your Body

1. Information on the woman's bodily changes are taken from the brochure "How Your Baby Grows: A Monthly Diary of Your Baby's Development," March of Dimes Defects Foundation, 2002.

2. La Leche League International, 1400 N. Meacham Road, Schaumburg, IL 60173-4808, 847-519-7730. www.lalecheleague.org gives information about contacting local groups.

3. "How Your Baby Grows."

Chapter Eleven: Stand Up Girl

1. Joe S. McIlhaney, M.D., brochure "Why Condoms Aren't Safe" (Colorado Springs: Focus on the Family, 1994).

2. Information about sexually transmitted diseases is from the Medical Institute for Sexual Health, Austin, Texas, www.medinstitute.org/medical/index.htm.

3. www.medinstitute.org/medical/STD%20overview/condoms+STDs.htm

Part Four: For Those You Love

Chapter Thirteen: For Your Baby's Father

1. Statutory rape laws are determined by individual states. They change from time to time. Some information is on the Internet; see www.sexlaws.org. You can also call the state legislature or local district attorney to ask what the law is.

Appendix A

1. "Making an Informed Decision about Your Pregnancy."

2. Adoption Choice unlimited is a Web site with links to information and help for birth mothers and prospective parents: www.adoptionchoiceunlimited.com.

3. Brochure "What about the Father? Rights, Duties, Responsibilities" (Fredericksburg, Va.: National Institute of Family & Life Advocates, 2004).

4. "What about the Father?"